STUDY GUIDE

James G. Duvall III
Contra Costa College

CULTURAL ANTHROPOLOGY

ELEVENTH EDITION

Carol R. Ember

Melvin Ember

PEARSON

Prentice
Hall

Upper Saddle River, New Jersey 07458

© 2004 by PEARSON EDUCATION, INC.
Upper Saddle River, New Jersey 07458

10 9 8 7 6 5 4 3 2 1

ISBN 0-13-111640-1

Printed in the United States of America

CONTENTS

To

Carlos Murillo-Martinez

Thanks for jumping into the fray
and
Helping in so many ways

PREFACE

A STUDY GUIDE TO ACCOMPANY <u>CULTURAL ANTHROPOLOGY</u>, eleventh edition, contains nineteen chapters for the student who is new to the field of cultural anthropology. Each chapter is designed to help involve the student in material by challenging him or her at various levels of thinking. As the text is arranged topically, so is the study guide. The purpose, then, is to move the student through a series of experiences that will lead him or her to fully appreciate the complexity of cultural variation across the world.

This is a classic survey course, therefore in a rather short amount of time, (one semester), the student is exposed to a large amount of jargon. Because of this, the study guide emphasizes the glossary terms and asks the student to define them *in the context of the chapter*. Another feature of the study guide is its use of the chapter boxes. Many excellent examples are contained in these. The student has the opportunity to utilize the information of the chapter by applying it to these examples.

While the textbook deals with general concepts and topics in anthropology, this study guide works to give the student hands-on experience with the concepts. Use of the study guide should greatly aid in the development of cultural and analytical skills that span many subject areas.

A NOTE TO THE INSTRUCTOR

A STUDY GUIDE TO ACCOMPANY <u>CULTURAL</u> <u>ANTHROPOLOGY</u>, eleventh edition, is a learner-centered, flexible workbook program, which allows a range of activities to be directed by you.

Your skill at communicating cultural information to your students should only be enhanced by the exercises that follow. This study guide closely follows the text -- so much so, in fact, that many of the exercises are based upon boxes in the individual chapters. Whenever possible, questions are posed relating to the **<u>Research Frontiers and Current Issues,</u> <u>New Perspectives on Gender</u>**, and **<u>Applied Anthropology</u>** boxes in the chapters.

Flexibility has been designed into each chapter. You may assign all or part of each chapter. Some parts may be assigned as homework, while some may be used for in-class group work.

Finally, the **Test Your Knowledge** section at the end of each chapter is designed to help your students know if they are learning the material. Essay questions are included in each test. These would make excellent group discussion questions and, of course, help in developing their writing skills.

A NOTE TO THE STUDENT

Study guide work is designed to help you better understand basic principles and concepts in anthropology. You will also gain a certain amount of experience applying common information and data to complex cultural and humanistic questions. Many of the exercises you will do require a synthetic approach, bringing data and theory together, to better understand the overall problem. It is the goal of the study guide that by providing you with so many problems, you will become more knowledgeable of cultural variation around the world.

This study guide is organized into thirty chapters that closely follow the text. Each chapter is set up in the following manner:

Chapter Outline -- A detailed outline of what the text chapter covers.

Major Points for Review -- Chapter Summary -- A short description of the general goals and ideas of the text chapter.

Defining the Glossary Terms -- A list of terms, which are context specific. In other words, terms which would have cultural meaning in the context of the topic being discussed in the chapter. It would greatly benefit you to become familiar with them. Please define them *in the context of the chapter.*

Check Your Understanding -- These are essentially essay questions. Many of them would be good for group work or discussion. They are almost all linked to chapter boxes such as the *Research Frontiers*, *Current Issues*, and *New Perspectives on Gender* included in the chapters.

Test Your Knowledge -- A short quiz that tests the learning objectives of the chapter. You may correct these yourself. The key is at the end of the study guide. Essay questions are also provided for you to develop your writing skills.

When you have completed this course, you should have a much greater knowledge of human culture. By studying each of these topics we get away from the sterile definition and see the entire world of diversity spread before us. You will hopefully gain a greater appreciation of what it is to be human.

CHAPTER 1: *What Is Anthropology?*

CHAPTER OUTLINE

I   The Scope of Anthropology

II   The Holistic Approach

III The Anthropological Curiosity

IV   Fields of Anthropology
     A. Biological Anthropology
     B. Cultural Anthropology
        1. Archaeology
        2. Anthropological Linguistics
        3. Ethnology

V   Applied Anthropology

VI   Specialization

VII The Relevance of Anthropology

MAJOR POINTS FOR REVIEW - CHAPTER SUMMARY

This chapter is introductory in nature. It develops the major theme found throughout the book that humans are infinitely curious about themselves. The scope of anthropology is very broad in that it studies humans from anywhere and from any time period. Other disciplines are heavily involved in studying the behavior of humans, but in a narrower context.

The discipline of anthropology takes in all forms of information that have to do with the behavior of humans. Because of this, anthropology is holistic in its approach. It is through this approach that we can satisfy our great curiosity as to why humans are motivated to do things as they do.

Anthropology, in its holistic approach, takes into account both cultural and biological information. The two major fields of anthropology are physical anthropology and cultural anthropology. Cultural anthropology is further subdivided into the fields of archaeology, anthropological linguistics, and ethnology. Each one of these fields leads to a greater understanding of the human condition throughout time and space. The synthesis of these sub fields allows anthropologists to develop a unique perspective in the understanding of human and cultural behavior.

Over the years, anthropologists have become more and more specialized. As our understanding of humans and human cultures have grown, so have the various specializations. Anthropologists have typically identified with one of the major subfields and some geographic region of the world. Commonly, however, anthropologists identify themselves by their study of humans in relationship to a certain academic discipline, such as economic anthropology, political anthropology, or psychology anthropology, etc. In this way they may study many societies in relationship to the sub field in which they specialize.

Applied anthropology is a newer area of expertise. Very much like the difference between pure and applied sciences, the field of applied anthropology takes modern day problems and analyzes them using the tools of all of the major fields of anthropology. In a very real sense, anthropology becomes a practical discipline for the solving of major problems that occur on a nearly daily basis in our ever-shrinking world.

The usefulness of anthropology is great. By helping us understand ourselves, anthropology helps avoid misunderstandings between peoples. Behavior that seemed strange to us may now make sense. By studying the people of the world, anthropology has found that the many differences between them are the result of physical and cultural adaptations to different environments. In simpler terms, people are people.

DEFINING THE GLOSSARY TERMS

Check your understanding of Chapter 1 by defining each of the glossary terms.

Anthropological linguistics   anthropological study of languages

Anthropology   a discipline that studies humans, focusing on the differences & similarities (biological Also cultural) in human populations (all times & all places in world)

Applied (practicing) anthropology   - to acheive practical goals. Outside academia

Archaeology   - branch of anth - seeks to reconstruct daily life & customs of peoples in past & to explain & trace cultural changes. (usually nothing written → reconstruction from material remains)

Biological (physical) anthropology   - study of humans as biological organisms deals with emergence & EVOLUTION & with contemporary biological variations.

Cross-cultural researcher   - ethnologist who uses ethnographic data about many societies to test possible explanations of cultural variation

Cultural anthropology – the study of cultural variation & universals.

Culture – the set of learned behaviours, beliefs, attitudes, values & ideals characteristic of a particular society or population.

Descriptive (structural) linguistics – study of how languages are constructed

Ethnographer – a person who spends some time living with, interviewing & observing a group of people to describe their customs

Ethnography a description of a society's customary behaviours, beliefs & attitudes.

Ethnohistorian – an ethnologist who uses historical documents to study how a culture has changed over time.

Ethnology – the study of how & why recent cultures differ & are similar

Fossils – the hardened remains or impressions of plants & animals that lived in the past.

Historical archaeology – a specialty w/in arch that studies the material remains of recent peoples who left written records.

Historical linguistics study of how languages change over time.

Holistic – refers to an approach that studies MANY aspects of a multifaceted system

Homo sapiens biological species to which all living people belong. All human populations on earth can interbreed. First homo sapiens 100,000 years ago.

Human paleontology OR PALEOANTHROPOLOGY
– the study of the emergence of humans & their later physical evolution.

Human variation – study of how & why contemporary human populations vary biologically

Paleoanthropology

Biological anthropology

Prehistory – the time before written records.

Primates – member of mammalian order. Divided into 2 suborders ⟨ prosimians / anthropoids.

Primatologists – persons who study primates.

Sociolinguistics – the study of cultural & subcultural patterns of speaking in different social contexts.

CHECK YOUR UNDERSTANDING

1. Refer to the *Research Frontiers* box on Elizabeth M. Brumfiel (page 6 of the text). What is the "benefit" explanation referred to here? What new discovery did she make in reference to this explanation? How did Elizabeth Brumfiel contribute to the community in which she did her field work?

   → S.O.L

   'benefit'-That inequality provided benefits to society (eg: standard of living of most people improved as leaders got richer)
   - Found little improvement in S.O.L of local people after Aztecs absorbed them

2. Refer to the *Applied Anthropology* box on Getting Development Programs to Notice Women's Contributions to Agriculture (page 9 of the text). What did Anita Spring study in Malawi? What was the purpose of the mini-projects? — Medical Anth.

   Studied customary healing practices involving women & children

   Mini-projects- so successful training techniques could be passed on to development agents in other regions.

3. Refer to the *Research Frontiers and Current Issues* box on Terence E. Hays (page 8 of the text). How did he test his ideas on mythology and cultural themes?

4. How does the holistic approach lead to a better understanding of human behavior? Is any one subfield of anthropology better at leading to a better understanding of human behavior than others? Explain your answer.

TEST YOUR KNOWLEDGE

Select the best answer for the multiple choice questions and circle the letter T *for true and* F *for false. Short answer essay questions should be answered in full sentences and as concisely as possible.*

1. Anthropology is the field that deals with the study of (p. 2)
    a. human history.
    b. primate psychology.
    c. the human environment.
    d. humans.

2. The _____ approach covers all aspects of a subject. (p. 2)
    a. humanistic
    b. hypothetical
    c. holistic
    d. historical

3. Which field of anthropology deals with the emergence of humans? (p. 4)
    a. Ethnology
    b. Ethnography
    c. Archaeology
    d. Paleoanthropology

4. Lacking written records, _____ must try to reconstruct history from the remains of human cultures. (p. 5)
    a. archaeologists
    b. ethnologists
    c. ethnographers
    d. paleoanthropologists

5. The field of _____ attempts to make anthropological knowledge useful. (p. 8)
    a. archaeology
    b. applied anthropology
    c. ethnology
    d. ethnography

6. T F An ethnographer may live with a group of people for a year or longer to determine the customary behavior of the group. (p. 7)

7. T F Specialties, in the field of anthropology, are produced in order to isolate anthropologists from other kinds of research. (p. 10)

8. T F Leslie White suggests that the reason for the late development of anthropology is because we humans tend to think of ourselves as citadels of free will and therefore find the study of human behavior too difficult to comprehend. (p. 10)

9. T **F** Anthropology is only useful in that it allows us to objectively view our past mistakes. (p. 2-12)

10. **T** F Anthropological linguistics studies the historical and descriptive or structural nature of language. (p. 5)

11. T **F** African American school children do not drink milk as readily as most children because they can not afford to buy it. (p. 2)

12. T **F** Anita Spring, while working in Malawi, studied male and female participation in agriculture and found that men commonly work harder than women in the fields. (p. 9)

13. **T** F Applied or practicing anthropology is explicit in its concern with making anthropological knowledge useful. (p. 8)

WRITE ABOUT WHAT YOU HAVE READ

14. What is the holistic approach of anthropology? How has it changed from the past to the present?

15. Describe the two sub fields of biological anthropology. Describe the three subfields of cultural anthropology. What is it that unifies all of these sub fields under the discipline of anthropology?

7

16. What is the usefulness of applied anthropology?

17. How can modern anthropological studies be used to help with modern social problems?

18. Compare and contrast ethnology with ethnography.

CHAPTER 2: *The Concept of Culture*

CHAPTER OUTLINE

I   Defining Features of Culture
    A. Culture is Commonly Shared
    B. Culture is Learned
        1. Language

II   Attitudes that Hinder the Study of Culture

III Cultural Relativism

IV. Describing a Culture
    A. Individual Variation
    B. Cultural Constraints
    C. Ideal versus Actual Cultural Patterns
    D. How to Discover Cultural Patterns

V   Some Assumptions about Culture
    A. Culture is Generally Adaptive
    B. Culture is Mostly Integrated
    C. Culture is Always Changing

MAJOR POINTS FOR REVIEW - CHAPTER SUMMARY

This is a key chapter in the text. It not only deals with the concept of culture but also introduces the reader to the major concepts of ethnocentrism and cultural relativity. While the former holds that your own society is the only one that makes sense, the latter concept allows us to view cultural customs outside of our experience in the context of the society which has it. This gives us a broader view of humanity and may even give rise to alternate solutions to problems inside of our own culture. While ethnocentrism may lead to inter-group conflict, cultural relativity should lead to a greater understanding of the needs and values of other societies. Cultural relativity is also in the center of the debate about human rights. Do we (Westerners) have the right to challenge other society's code of ethics, which obviously are dissimilar to ours? A strict following of cultural relativity would stop the Western world from interceding in human rights violations. So perhaps cultural relativity is too inflexible and needs to be rethought.

A simple definition of culture is that it is the total way of life of a society. By definition this would mean that cultural elements are shared commonly throughout the society. When only a group inside of the society shares some customs, we are referring to a subculture. Cultural items are also learned. Almost all human behavior falls into this category. This is exactly why humans are referred to as cultural animals. Genetically determined traits such as eye or hair color are not cultural. How one combs his/her hair or applies makeup to the eyes is cultural. Culture is transmitted from one individual to another through language. Human language is symbolic. Language is symbolic in that a word or phrase can represent what something stands for whether or not that thing is present.

The authors next develop the problems anthropologists have in describing cultures. Anthropologists look for commonalties in a society. While individual variation in behavior exist, the behaviors fall within a set of limits. It is these limits that anthropologists look for. In effect they are attempting to discover the customs and the ranges of acceptable behavior that characterize the society under study. Emile Durkheim stressed that culture is something outside of us. Culture exerts a strong coercive force that constrains our behavior. The constraints he refers to come in two types: direct and indirect. Direct constraints tend to be tied up with law or strong customs. Indirect constraints are just as compelling, yet the behavior, while not required, is certainly enforced, possibly because the individual will not have the ability to perform whatever action it is that he or she would like. Culture is next described as how societies view themselves versus how they really act. This is ideal versus actual cultural patterns. Actual cultural patterns are the result of the above mentioned constraints. If everyone acted ideally then cultural constraints would be unnecessary.

How anthropologists discover cultural patterns is of some concern. Two types of patterns are of importance: those that are overt, or easily seen by the anthropologist and those that the people being studied are unaware of. In the latter case some form of sampling of individual behavior would be necessary in order to establish a pattern.

Finally, other elements of culture are developed. Culture is generally adaptive. Simply put, this means that cultural traits or customs help the society adapt to its environment and therefore lead to the survival of the society. Culture is mostly integrated. Since most cultural traits are adaptive, it follows that they rest one upon another. Customs and traits are not just a random assortment where the religion, for instance, is not in any way related to the language. Another example would be the relationship of economic systems to methods of food production. One last feature of culture is that it is always changing. Since the function of a cultural system is to help the society adapt to its environment, then the culture must always be changing in order to meet its needs.

DEFINING THE GLOSSARY TERMS

Check your understanding of Chapter 2 by defining each of the glossary terms.

Adaptive   customs that enhance survival & reproductive success

Culture relativism   to look at a [society's customs & ideas] e in the context of it's problems & opportunities

Culture the set of learned behaviours. beliefs, attitudes values & ideals characteristic of a particular society or population.

Early evolutionism – view that culture develops in a uniform & progressive manner

Ethnocentric – judgement of other cultures solely in terms of one's own.

Ethnocentrism the attitude of

Maladaptive customs – customs that diminish survival & reproductive success.

Norms – standards or rules about acceptable behaviour in a society
– importance can be judged by how members of a society respond when norm is violated.

Random sample – sample in which all cases included have had an equal chance to be included.

Society – a group of people who occupy a particular territory & speak a common language not generally understood by neighbouring peoples. Do not necessarily correspond to nations.

Subculture – Shared customs of a subgroup w/in a society.

CHECK YOUR UNDERSTANDING

1. Refer to the *Research Frontiers and Current Issues* box titled "Human Rights and Cultural Relativity." How can the concept of cultural relativism and an international standard for individual human rights be reconciled? (This is definitely your own opinion.)

2. Refer to the *Portraits of Culture* box titled "The Nandi of Kenya." How did Regina Smith and her husband Leon deal with their own ethnocentrism in this example? How do you interpret the fact that Kenyan's are less tolerant of homosexuality than North Americans in light of their touching behavior?

3. Refer to the *Applied Anthropology* box titled "Why the Bedouin Do Not Readily Settle Down." What conflicts arise between traditional culture and the desires of the government for change?

4. Think about the culture referred to in the book as the North American Culture. Select a trait that you feel is maladaptive. Describe the trait. What about it is maladaptive? What could be done "fix" the trait (problem)? How could the new trait you have invented be enforced?

5. Emile Durkheim has described two basic types of cultural constraints. What are they? Give examples for each type from your own experience.

DIRECT & INDIRECT

12

TEST YOUR KNOWLEDGE

Select the best answer for the multiple choice questions and circle the letter T *for true and* F *for false. Short answer essay questions should be answered in full sentences and as concisely as possible.*

1. When a person judges a custom of another society solely in terms of his or her own cultural values he or she is being (p. 17)
   a. egocentric.
   b. relativistic.
   c. ethnocentric.
   d. barbaric.

2. Cultural _____ asks that all customs be viewed _____, not ethnocentrically or romantically. (p. 19)
   a. relativism, subjectively
   b. relativism, objectively
   c. materialism, subjectively
   d. materialism, scientifically

3. When a subgroup in a society shares customs that the larger society does not, then a (p. 15)
   a. poliety exists.
   b. political part has been established.
   c. neutral viewpoint exists.
   d. subculture exists.

4. Humans _____ almost all of their behavior and therefore must use language as a method of transmitting information symbolically. (p. 16)
   a. inherit
   b. learn
   c. share
   d. create

5. According to Emile Durkheim, culture is a(n) _____ force and _____ us from exhibiting too much individual cultural variation. (p. 21)
   a. evil, forces
   b. constraining, stops
   c. coercive, constrains
   d. indirect, constrains

6. (T) F The statement 'culture is generally adaptive,' means that cultural traits help the people of a society adapt the environment to the needs of the society. (p. 24)

7. T (F) All cultural traits must help the society adapt to a given environmental condition. (p. 24)

8. (T) F An attitude of superiority by a member of one society about the practices of another is ethnocentrism. (p. 17)

9. T F The concept of cultural relativism means that cultural traits inside of a society can not be valued or judged more or less than any others. (p. 19)

10. (T) F Although the variations in individual reactions to a given stimulus are theoretically limitless, in fact they tend to fall within easily recognizable limits. (p. 20)

11. T (F) The modern view of cultural relativism is that no country should intervene in another country's practices, no matter what rights are being violated. (p. 19)

12. T (F) Bedouin animal grazing and new government settlements have increased the productivity of Bedouin herding. (p. 25)

13. (T) F The tendency for a culture to be integrated may be cognitively and emotionally induced. (p. 26)

WRITE ABOUT WHAT YOU HAVE READ

14. How does the concept of cultural relativism help you deal with your own ethnocentrism?

15. What is culture? How is it transmitted? What is a subculture? How do subcultures relate to the larger culture?

16. How does culture constrain individuals from being completely free to do anything they want to do?

17. Describe the two possible processes for the elimination of maladaptive cultural customs using your own examples for these customs.

18. Why is a forced change in the religion of a society such a destructive event?

CHAPTER 3: *Theory and Evidence in Cultural Anthropology*

CHAPTER OUTLINE

I   Theoretical Orientations
   A. Cultural Ecology
   B. Political Economy: World System Theory
   C. Sociobiology and Behavioral Ecology
   D. Interpretive Approaches

II   Explanation
   A. Association or Relationships
   B. Theories

III   Why Theories Cannot Be Proved

IV   Generating Theories

V   Evidence: Testing Explanations
   A. Operationalization and Measurement
   B. Sampling
   C. Statistical Evaluation

VI   Types of Research in Cultural Anthropology
   A. Ethnography
   B. Within-Culture Comparisons
   C. Regional Controlled Comparisons
   D. Cross-Cultural Research
   E. Historical Research

MAJOR POINTS FOR REVIEW - CHAPTER SUMMARY

Over the last century, anthropologists have collected an awful lot of facts. This chapter deals with the various ways in which they are organized. As is evident from the above outline, there are numerous methods for dealing with facts in anthropology. When they are assembled into a model or pattern of reality, we call that pattern a theory. The many methods are listed above. So, in effect, these various systems for assembling facts are the many theoretical approaches anthropologists take in the attempt to understand human cultural behavior.

The approach labeled cultural ecology was first proposed by Julian Steward. He separated cultural ecology from biological ecology. Later, Roy Rappaport and Andrew Vadya integrated the two areas into one field: ecology. In this view, cultural traits, just like biological traits, can be adaptive or maladaptive.

Political economy explains social change because of external forces also. This approach discounts the social and natural environment and suggests that the social and political impact of powerful state societies is the central factor in social change and adaptation.

Sociobiology or behavioral ecology is similar to cultural ecology. This approach is mostly the invention of biologists and focuses on individual behavior and adaptation rather than the adaptation of the group to its environment, as in cultural ecology. It is the individual who must adapt to the environment (through behavior) or he or she will not be able to pass on his or her genes and thus not be able to pass on his or her behavior (through learning).

Clifford Geertz has proposed the idea that a culture is like a literary text that can be analyzed for meaning, as the ethnographer interprets it. This approach espouses that interpretation is the only achievable goal of ethnography and that no one can describe cultural behavior in objective scientific terms.

Many modern anthropologists would deny any particular theoretical approach to their studies. Rather, they use hypothesis testing to try to explain cultural behavior. Any theory may have useful parts. They feel that in the absence of testing, any conclusions reached should be viewed skeptically.

One of the goals of anthropology is explanation, or the answer to a "why" question. One way to answer why questions is through the association of two variables. By going through the process of explanation scientists generate theories. Theories are more complex than an association. Some parts of theories cannot ever be observed. It is because of this last statement that theories can never be proved. While they may be based on factual data and evidence, no theory can be said to be unquestionably true.

How anthropologists generate theories is the next focus in this chapter. The authors suggest two possible methods: single-case analysis and comparing different societies that share a particular characteristic. This section points out that only plausible relationships need be investigated, not the entire body of anthropological knowledge.

How anthropologists test explanations is important. It is the quantitative portion of anthropology that uses operationalization, measurement, sampling, and statistical analysis to test explanations. By doing this, anthropologists literally keep testing their beliefs against sets of objective evidence that could falsify those same beliefs.

The research anthropologists perform varies tremendously depending upon the spatial and temporal scope of the study. Spatial scope refers to how many societies are to be studied while temporal scope refers to whether the study is historical or nonhistorical. The various combinations of these two possibilities lead to ethnography, within-culture comparisons, nonhistorical comparisons, cross-cultural research, and historical research.

DEFINING THE GLOSSARY TERMS

Check your understanding of Chapter 3 by defining each of the glossary terms.

Behavioral ecology

Cultural ecology

Explanation

Falsification

Fieldwork

Group selection

Hypotheses

Individual selection

Laws

Measure

Operational definition

Participant-observation

Political economy

Probability value (p-value)

Sampling universe

Sociobiology

Statistical association

Statistically significant

Theoretical construct

Theories

Variables

CHECK YOUR UNDERSTANDING

1. Compare the various types of research in anthropology: ethnography, within-culture comparisons, nonhistorical controlled comparisons, cross-cultural research, and historical research. Also note at what level they are in a spatial and temporal context.

2. Refer to the *Research Frontiers and Current Issues* box titled "Fieldwork: How Can We Know What is True?" What is the value of fieldwork? What is the controversy that surrounds the work of Margaret Mead's study in Samoa? What is the explanation that Paul Shankman proposes to answer the questions raised by Freeman?

3. Select a modern urban center in America (a major city). What sociological problem would you like to study? How would you set up the study? What type of research approach would you take? Why?

4. Refer to the *Research Frontiers and Current Issues* box titled "Evaluating Alternative Theories." What is the connection between yams and sex discovered by Richard Scaglion when he studied the Abelam of New Guinea? How does theory in anthropology help in understanding this connection and others?

TEST YOUR KNOWLEDGE

Select the best answer for the multiple choice questions and circle the letter T *for true and* F *for false. Short answer essay questions should be answered in full sentences and as concisely as possible.*

1. An explanation is an answer to a _____ question. (p. 33)
   a. where
   b. what
   c. how
   d. why

2. To _____ something is to say how it compares with other things on some scale of variation. (p. 38)
   a. explain
   b. produce
   c. measure
   d. define

3. A(n) _____ sample is one in which all cases selected had an equal chance to be included. (p. 38)
   a. statistical
   b. random
   c. covariant
   d. population

4. The _____ is the likelihood that the observed result or a stronger one could have occurred by chance. (p. 39)
   a. statistical mean
   b. median
   c. p-value
   d. t-value

5. After doing fieldwork, an anthropologist may prepare a (p. 40)
   a. controlled-comparison.
   b. ethnography.
   c. regional controlled comparison.
   d. cross-cultural research.

6. T F A political economist discounts the effect of the natural environment on the formation of current societies. (p. 31)

7. T F Sociobiology, like cultural ecology, sees cultural traits as being adaptive or maladaptive. The difference lies in that sociobiologists view characteristics as being adaptive for the individual in a given environment. (p. 32)

8. T F Falsification is the main way theories are judged. (p. 36)

9. T F As theories are based on factual evidence, they themselves are quite provable. (p. 36)

10. T F Creating explanations for associations is a method for creating theories. (p. 35)

11. T F The sampling universe is always the widest possible population. (p. 38)

12. T F Participant observation is considered to be the best method for developing ethnographic information. (p. 40)

13. T F In a regional controlled comparison, the anthropologist compares ethnographic information obtained from societies found in a particular region. (p. 43)

WRITE ABOUT WHAT YOU HAVE READ

14. What is central to the approach taken by political economists? What is the argument this approach has with cultural ecology?

15. What is cross-cultural research? What is this technique used for? If the sample is taken randomly what value do the results have?

16. What is a theory? Why can they not be proved?

17. What is an operational definition? How did John Whiting define the first variable? How is classification a form of measurement?

18. Why is random sampling so important to scientific research?

19. What is ethnography? What are the difficulties with participant observation?

CHAPTER 4: *Communication and Language*

CHAPTER OUTLINE

I   Communication
  A. Nonverbal Human Communication
  B. Nonhuman Communication

II The Origins of Language
  A. Creole Languages
  B. Children's Acquisition of Language

III Descriptive Linguistics
  A. Phonology
  B. Morphology
  C. Syntax

IV Historical Linguistics
  A. Language Families and Culture History

V   The Processes of Linguistic Divergence

VI Relationships between Language and Culture
  A. Cultural Influences on Language
  B. Linguistic Influences on Culture: The Sapir-Whorf Hypothesis

VII The Ethnography of Speaking
  A. Social Status and Speech
  B. Gender Differences in Speech
  C. Multilingualism and Codeswitching

MAJOR POINTS FOR REVIEW - CHAPTER SUMMARY

This chapter deals with communication. Humans, for the most part, communicate with language. Other animal species also communicate in various ways. While human language is completely symbolic, so are some other primates to a much lesser extent. More importantly, our system of language is open, in other words, it allows for new utterances to be created by combining sounds using complex rules of grammar and syntax to produce an infinite array of meanings.

The authors next discuss the origins of human language. They point out one idea that vocal language is no older than our species as a result of anatomical differences with our earlier ancestors. Another point of view is that having an open communication system would be a favorable adaptation to an ever-changing environment. A language acquisition device in the brain is even hypothesized. This device would force the learning of language by all humans, rather than the inheritance of fixed calls. Studies of the many languages of humans by anthropologists does indicate that their are no primitive languages. All human societies have equally complex systems of language.

The study of structural (descriptive) linguistics is an important part of this chapter. Anthropological linguists have devised methods of studying any language by examining its structure. In doing so the linguist tries to discover the rules of phonology (the patterning of sounds), morphology (the patterning of sound sequences and words), and syntax (the patterning of phrases and sentences) that predict how most speakers of a language will talk.

Linguists are also very interested in how languages have changed over time. These historical linguists can even reconstruct non-written languages by comparing them to other similar contemporary languages. An example would be the comparison of Finnish and Hungarian, both having the same origin in the Urals, long since having diverged.

Two basic ideas about the relationship between language and culture are presented in the text. One is the cultural influence on language best seen in the vocabulary (lexical context) of a society. Less agreed upon is the concept that language has some effect upon the culture. The Sapir-Whorf hypothesis states that language is a force in its own right - that it affects how individuals in a society perceive and conceive reality.

Sociolinguistics is the last topic covered in this chapter. Sociolinguistics is the study of the variation in the way people of a society speak. Sociolinguists are concerned with what one speaks about in various situations, and how one speaks to various individuals depending upon social status.

DEFINING THE GLOSSARY TERMS

Check your understanding of Chapter 4 by defining each of the glossary terms.

Codeswitching   using more than one language in the course of conversing

Cognates   words or morphs that belong to different languages but have similar sounds & meanings

Core vocabulary   - non-specialist vocabulary

Dialects   - varieties of languages spoken in particular areas or by particular social groups.

Historical linguistics *Study of how langs change over time*

Lexical content *— vocabulary or lexicon*

Lexicon *— the words & morphs, and their meanings, of a language; approximated by the dictionary*

Morph

Morpheme

Morphology

Phone

Phonemes

Phonology

Protolanguage

Syntax

CHECK YOUR UNDERSTANDING

1. What are the various ways in which animals (including humans) communicate? How is human language open while other animals basically have closed systems of communication?

2. Refer to the *Applied Anthropology* box titled "Can Languages Be Kept From Extinction?" What percentage of languages arc in danger of being lost? Describe the two proposals that are being tried to "rescue" nearly extinct languages. Do you think one is better than the other? If so, why?

3. Refer to the *New Perspectives on Gender* box titled "Does the English Language Promote Sexist Thinking?". What form does sexism take in the English language? How does the Sapir-Whorf hypothesis relate to this topic? What are the current solutions to sexist phraseology in English?

TEST YOUR KNOWLEDGE

Select the best answer for the multiple choice questions and circle the letter T *for true and* F *for false. Short answer essay questions should be answered in full sentences and as concisely as possible.*

1. The term symbolic, when used in conjunction with language (p. 49)
   a. means that symbols are used to produce writing.
   b. means that the symbols are arbitrary and can be used outside the presence of the referent.
   c. means that any meaning is acceptable inside of the language.
   d. refers to the chimpanzee and gorilla call systems.

2. A morph is (p. 56)
   a. a small unit of sound.
   b. just a small version of a morpheme.
   c. the smallest unit of language that has a meaning.
   d. synonymous with the term phone.

3. A _____ is a series of sounds that do not make any difference in meaning. (p. 54)
   a. morpheme
   b. morph
   c. phone
   d. phoneme

4. _____ are words that are similar in sound and meaning from different languages. (p. 58)
   a. Morphs
   b. Cognates
   c. Phones
   d. Morphemes

5. The Sapir-Whorf hypothesis states that (p. 62)
   a. language exerts great influence on culture.
   b. language affects how individuals in a society perceive and conceive reality.
   c. language is influenced heavily by the environment.
   d. culture is the key determinant in how language is formed.

6. T F Social status has very little to do with how people speak to each other. (p. 63)

7. T F Codeswitching is a method of purposely confusing other listeners in a conversation. (p. 66)

8. T F Proto-Indo-European most likely originated in the Indus-Ganges river valleys. (p. 58)

9. T F A phone is a small unit of sound that when grouped with other phones which sound alike make up a phoneme. (p. 54)

10. T F Odor is a major communication style of many animals. (p. 49)

WRITE ABOUT WHAT YOU HAVE READ

11. How is body movement used in animal communication?

12. How do social forces shape dialect differences in the same language at the same location?

13. What are the stages of language acquisition for children? Why do children all over the world tend to progress to the same stages at the same ages?

14. What is Dick Bickerton's argument based on Creole language?

15. What is the Sapir-Whorf hypothesis? How does the development of gender identity
    in children support this hypothesis?

CHAPTER 5: *Getting Food*

CHAPTER OUTLINE

MAJOR POINTS FOR REVIEW - CHAPTER SUMMARY

Getting food is a chapter devoted to the various techniques humans employ or have employed in the procurement of their daily nutrition. In other words, this chapter is about the universal quest of all humans to meet there most basic of all needs: nutrition. While all organisms have this very same need, only humans have such a large number of techniques for getting their food.

Basically, food can either be collected or produced. The amount of variation inside of each category is staggering. The authors almost exhaustively explore every technique. Food collection is defined as all subsistence technology in which food getting is dependent on naturally occurring resources-that is, wild plants and animals. Humans have lived this way for almost all of history; only recently has the population turned away from it. As the Pleistocene (ice ages) came to a close, people in various parts of the world turned to food production.

Food collection revolves around hunting, gathering, and fishing. Different cultures rely more or less heavily on these resources depending upon environmental conditions. In societies where hunting or fishing produces most of the food, men provide most of the calories for the group. In societies where collecting provides most of the food, women provide most of the calories. The cultural consequences of collecting food are: collectors would live in low-density population regions, be extremely nomadic, own no more than they could carry, not recognize property ownership, and have a division of labor based upon gender and age, rather than class.

Food production techniques show some of the greatest variation of anything that humans do. Horticulture is the growing of all crops with simple tools, in the absence of permanently cultivated fields, such as shifting cultivation. Intensive agriculture, on the other hand, is much more complex. This agricultural technique is used on permanent fields, with the use of complex tools, such as plows, draft animals, and fertilizers, to replace the nutrients taken out of the fields by the crops. As intensive agriculture has intensified, it has become commercialized in much of the world. While intensive agriculturalists grow most of their food for consumption, commercial agriculturalists grow most their food for sale. As more of food production has become commercialized, fewer people are involved in the production of food. The final form of food production is pastoralism. It involves the domestication of animals. In most cases, pastoralism is not for the slaughter of animals but rather for the use of animal products such as milk blood, wool, or hair. The direct cultural consequences of food production is that people not only own land, but also live at least semi-permanently in one place and thus own much more than a hunter-gatherer ever could. Labor becomes specialized, so that not everyone can do everything. Not everyone farms for a living anymore and wealth is no longer equally distributed. Cities can come into existence at this point because of surpluses. Political organization is well beyond the family and even the village. State-level societies have all been based on agriculture.

What role does the physical environment play in all of this? Anthropologists have concluded that the environment restrains certain activities rather than determines them. While no one grows crops in the arctic, food production in the forms of pastoralism and collection are both practiced in this hostile environment. Many deserts are now farmed due to high technology irrigation schemes, similar to the system utilized in the state of California.

The question of why cultures turned to food production is asked last in this chapter. If food collecting was so successful, then why change to a system that requires so much more work? Simply put, people were pushed into it. The authors give three separate hypotheses explaining how: 1. Population growth in good areas pushed people into marginal areas. They were forced to grow foods to survive. 2. Global population growth forced people into marginal regions, once again. This led to the domestication of plants and animals. 3. A drying climate at the end of the Pleistocene caused people of formerly lush areas to now be living in near deserts. Horticulture was the only answer to this problem.

DEFINING THE GLOSSARY TERMS

Check your understanding of Chapter 5 by defining each of the glossary terms.

Cash crop

Commercialization

Extensive or shifting cultivation

Food collection

Food production

Foragers

Horticulture

Hunter-gatherers

Intensive agriculture

Pastoralism

Prairie

Savanna

Slash-and-burn

Steppe

CHECK YOUR UNDERSTANDING

1. Refer to the New Perspectives on Gender box titled "From Man the Hunter to Woman the Gatherer, to...?". What makes fishing the most important form of food collection? What is it about both books, "Man the Hunter," and "Woman the Gatherer," that makes them both biased?

2. Review Table 5-1 (page 71). Which group (defined by how they get or produce their food) has the highest population density? The lowest? Why? Why do horticulturalists generally have less trouble with food shortages than either pastoralists or intensive agriculturalists?

3. Refer to the *Current Issues* box titled "The Effect of Food-Getting on the Environment," What is the biggest environmental problem with irrigation? What was the experience of the Hohokam of Arizona? How does this relate to the San Joaquin Valley of California?

TEST YOUR KNOWLEDGE

Select the best answer for the multiple choice questions and circle the letter T for true and F for false. Short answer essay questions should be answered in full sentences and as concisely as possible.

1. Early foragers lived in what type of environment? (p. 69)
   a. All types
   b. Coastal
   c. Arid desert
   d. Dense tropical

2. Which of the following is not a general feature of food collection? (p. 71)
   a. Few possessions
   b. Extensive political system
   c. Nomadism
   d. Rare food shortages

3. _____ is a form of food production which employs simple tools and no draft animals. (p. 72-73)
   a. Agriculture
   b. Intensive agriculture
   c. Pastoralism
   d. Horticulture

4. What type of society cannot rely on their production alone but must trade with others? (p. 77)
   a. Agricultural
   b. Intensive agriculture
   c. Pastoralism
   d. Horticulture

5. What the Inupiaq collect for food depends mostly on the (p. 70)
   a. temperature.
   b. soil type.
   c. native animals.
   d. season.

6. T F Pastoralists face the very real possibility of food shortages, more so than a hunter-gatherer group. (p. 71)

7. T F As Yanamamo crops do not provide much protein they must raise domesticated animals for that purpose. (p. 73)

8. T F Samoans raise pigs and chickens for the majority of their animal protein. (p. 74)

9. T F In the United States today, less than 2% of the total population lives on farms. (p. 77)

10. T F Irrigation agriculture has led to the saltation of the soils of many societies in the past. Fortunately, newer technologies have solved this problem so that we do not face it. (p. 80)

WRITE ABOUT WHAT YOU HAVE READ

11. What are the three major reasons why we must be cautious about drawing inferences about past foragers from observations of present foragers?

12. What are the three major reasons for the switch to food production?

13. Describe the two major forms of pastoralism. Why must pastoralists always maintain ties to agriculturalists?

14. What is horticulture? What is shifting cultivation? How did the Samoans practice horticulture?

15. What are the major differences between horticulture and intensive agriculture? What sociological differences exist between the two?

CHAPTER 6: *Economic Systems*

CHAPTER OUTLINE

I   The Allocation of Resources
   A. Natural Resources: Land
      1. Food Collectors
      2. Horticulturalists
      3. Pastoralists
      4. Intensive Agriculturalists
      5. Colonialism, the State, and Land Rights
   B. Technology

II   The Conversion of Resources
   A. Types of Economic Production
   B. Incentives for Labor
   C. Forced Labor
   D. Division of Labor
      1. By Gender and Age
      2. Beyond Gender and Age
   E. The Organization of Labor
   F. Making Decisions about Work

III   The Distribution of Goods and Services
   A. Reciprocity
      1. Generalized Reciprocity
      2. Balanced Reciprocity
      3. The Kula Ring
      4. Kinship Distance and Type of Reciprocity
      5. Reciprocity as a Leveling Device
   B. Redistribution
   C. Market or Commercial Exchange
      1. Kinds of Money
   D. Degrees of Commercialization
   E. Why Do Money and Market Exchange Develop?
   F. Possible Leveling Devices in Commercial Economics

MAJOR POINTS FOR REVIEW - CHAPTER SUMMARY

Economics. When most Americans hear that term they think money. Yet all societies have economies while most have not used money as a medium of exchange. In fact, economics refers more to the regulation of access to natural resources. How people exchange goods and services is a second theme of this chapter, and finally the methods with which societies divide the labor resources are also explored.

Access to land resources varies depending upon the way a group of people makes their living. Hunter-gatherers and horticulturalists do not own land at the individual or family level. If land ownership happens at all, it is at the band or village level. While horticulturalists also do not own land on an individual basis they do own their animals. Intensive agriculturalists do own their own land. Since the practice of agriculture is sedentary, the land can be owned as the use of it continues, season after season.

The tools of the exploitation of economic resources become more complex as the society being studied goes from food collecting to intensive agriculture. While anyone can make the tools for horticulture, specialists make the tools for intensive agriculture. They must be purchased and become the private property of the purchaser.

Labor is divided in all societies by gender. Furthermore, as societies become more technological, food surpluses become more common, thus releasing many people from the role of food producer. This provides more people for specialized skills, making better tools and thus more productive farming, which then releases more people from food production. This is a positive feedback loop.

A large portion of this chapter is devoted to how economic resources are distributed. Three major systems exist. They are not mutually exclusive, many societies use all three. Reciprocity, redistribution, and market or commercial exchange are the basis of distribution throughout the world. Reciprocity involves the exchange of goods and or services. It may mean an immediate exchange in which case it would be balanced, or it may be that there is no expectation of an exchange. This is gift giving called generalized reciprocity. Finally, in an exchange where one party is clearly trying to get the best of a deal by cheating or stealing, the exchange is referred to as negative reciprocity.

Redistribution is another form of exchange found in all societies. The term refers to the way in which our taxes are collected and used, but also refers to the distribution of resources in a family or village.

Supply and demand controls the pricing of material goods and services in a market economy. This is the one system that almost requires the use of some form of money. While most money is all-purpose (or multi-purpose), some is of special use, meaning that it can only be used for purchasing a single item that may be in short supply. Today we are racing toward a single-market world with demand being the final arbiter of supply.

DEFINING THE GLOSSARY TERMS

Check your understanding of Chapter 6 by defining each of the glossary terms.

Balanced reciprocity

Corvée

Generalized reciprocity

General-purpose money

Kula ring

Market or commercial exchange

Optimal foraging theory

Peasants

Potlatch

Reciprocity

Redistribution

Special-purpose money

CHECK YOUR UNDERSTANDING

1. Refer to the *Applied Anthropology* box titled "Impact of the World-System---Deforestation of the Amazon.". What economic forces have led to the deforestation of portions of the Brazilian rain forest? How can the indigenous peoples of the rain forest exploit it without destroying it? Of what value are the rain forests to the rest of the world?

2. Refer to the *Research Frontiers and Current Issues* box titled "Does Communal Ownership Lead to Economic Disaster?". What is Garrett Hardin's conclusion about communal ownership? How do pastoralists and fishers prevent the degradation of their environment? In the final analysis, which group can do a better job of ownership: Private owners or communal owners?

3. Draw a simple table comparing the land-ownership patterns and technological base of the following economies: Food Collectors, Horticulturalists, Pastoralists, and Intensive Agriculturalists.

TEST YOUR KNOWLEDGE

Select the best answer for the multiple choice questions and circle the letter T *for true and* F *for false. Short answer essay questions should be answered in full sentences and as concisely as possible.*

1. Of the following economies, which allows the individual ownership of land? (p. 90)
    a. Food collectors
    b. Pastoralists
    c. Horticulturalists
    d. Intensive agriculturalists

2. Which group needs the highest level of technology in order to convert resources to food and other goods? (p. 91-92)
    a. Food collectors
    b. Pastoralists
    c. Horticulturalists
    d. Intensive agriculturalists

3. The distribution of goods and services by all societies can be classified in all but which type? (p. 97)
    a. Reciprocity
    b. Redistribution
    c. Lottery
    d. Market exchange

4. In a state-level society such as the United States, the payment of taxes represents (p. 95)
    a. a voluntary system of redistribution.
    b. a form of forced labor which involves massive redistribution.
    c. an involuntary system of forced labor where givers receive equal to their gifts.
    d. the wealth of the nation.

5. Universally, _____ and _____ and _____ and _____ do not do the same kind of work. (p. 95)
    a. men, women, adults, children
    b. men, women, peasants, landowners
    c. men, women, boys, girls
    d. older men, younger men, boys, girls

6. T F General-purpose money is often used for commercial transactions, but rarely is it used for non-commercial transactions. (p. 103)

7. T F Generalized reciprocity results in the exploitation of another individual in a trade. (p. 97-98)

8. T F The Kula ring is a trading practice of the south Andean Mountains people of Chile that involves trading stone rings for papayas. (p. 99-100)

9. T F Reciprocal gift-giving may act as a form of leveling device which means that all surpluses are absorbed by the local government and then redistributed. (p. 101)

10. T F Market exchange refers to supply and demand exchanges that occur in a market-place environment. (p. 102-103)

WRITE ABOUT WHAT YOU HAVE READ

11. What types of societies practice redistribution? In which societies is it important?

12. What is special-purpose money? Of what use was this type of money to Melanesians and Northwest Coast natives?

13. List and describe the three types of reciprocity. How does giving benefit the giver?

14. How do kinship distance and type of reciprocity compare?

15. How is reciprocity used as a leveling device? What is a potlatch? How is it used as a leveling device?

CHAPTER 7: *Social Stratification: Class, Racism, and Ethnicity*

CHAPTER OUTLINE

I   Variation in Degree of Social Inequality

II   Egalitarian Societies

III Rank Societies

IV Class Societies
   A. Open Class Systems
      1. Degrees of Openness
      2. Degree of Inequality
   B. Caste Systems
   C. Slavery

V   Racism and Inequality
   A. Race as a Construct in Biology
   B. Race as a Social Category

VI Ethnicity and Inequality

VII The Emergence of Stratification

MAJOR POINTS FOR REVIEW - CHAPTER SUMMARY

The focus of Chapter 7 is that of social stratification. Sociologists would normally show that stratification exists in all societies while anthropologists make quite clear distinctions between age grades and gender. Some societies are not stratified at all but are egalitarian, meaning that all people in the society have equal access to economic power and prestige resources, dependent only upon their age grade or gender.

In some societies people have equal access to economic resources and even power, but not prestige. These are rank societies and are quite often pastoral or horticultural. In others, all factors are unequally distributed. Economic resources, power, and rank are reserved for people of a particular group inside of the society. In many instances there is a sliding scale of who has these attributes. It is interesting to note that the three do not always go together. This is the class system, with a class being a group of people who have almost equal access to the above three factors. An open class system allows some mobility for members of one class to move to another class. This can be an upward or downward movement, although the movement into the upper class is generally restricted.

Closed class systems are called caste systems. Membership is controlled by birth. There is technically not supposed to be any mobility. You cannot marry outside of the group, and children cannot acquire another caste status. In most caste systems, the groupings are determined by occupation. Certain occupations garner more money, respect, and power than others. In this type of system every individual knows what is expected of him or her and is better satisfied with his or her role in the society. India's caste system is probably the most famous, but other societies have at least parts of caste systems. The United States, in the past, treated blacks as if they were in a lower caste group, the Japanese had the Eta, who functioned much as the untouchables of India, and in Rwanda the Tutsi's were the ruling caste, forcing the Hutu's to farm on Tutsi land. Other examples exist all over the world.

Why has stratification emerged over most of the world? Three theories exist to explain this phenomenon. One theory proposed by Marshall Sahlins, suggests that social stratification developed as productivity increased and surpluses were produced. Another states that stratification can only develop when people have investments in land or technology and therefore cannot move away from leaders they do not like. Finally, it is theorized by C. K. Meek that population pressure brings about differential access to economic resources.

DEFINING THE GLOSSARY TERMS

Check your understanding of Chapter 7 by defining each of the glossary terms.

Caste

Class

Class societies

Clines

Egalitarian societies

Ethnicity

Manumission

Races

Racism

Rank societies

Slaves

CHECK YOUR UNDERSTANDING

1. Refer to the *Applied Anthropology* box titled "Disparities in Death: African Americans Compared with European Americans.". What historical factors may have lead to an increase in poor health in the African American community? What possible explanations are there for the described differences?

2. How does slavery in ancient Greece compare to that in the Nupe society in central Nigeria?

3. Refer to the *Research Frontiers and Current Issues* box titled "Is Global Inequality Increasing?". How do the richest 20 percent of the countries compare to the poorest 20 percent (Use GNP, trade, savings, and investment for the comparison)?. How is it possible that while the richer countries become richer and the inequality between the richest fifth and the poorest fifth increases, the world economy has improved overall, and that all countries have improved over the last 30 years?

TEST YOUR KNOWLEDGE

Select the best answer for the multiple choice questions and circle the letter T for true and F for false. Short answer essay questions should be answered in full sentences and as concisely as possible.

1. The United States, Canada, and most European countries have social systems which anthropologists would label (p. 114)
   a. open caste systems.
   b. open class societies.
   c. closed class systems.
   d. rank societies.

2. In a(n) _____ society the members have equal access to economic resources, power, and prestige. (p. 109)
   a. rank
   b. class
   c. egalitarian
   d. caste

3. Most societies that are _____ practice agriculture or herding. (p. 111)
   a. class
   b. caste
   c. egalitarian
   d. rank

4. What two factors have been shown to determine the class level of Americans in various studies? (p. 113)
   a. education level and religion
   b. education level and wealth
   c. occupation and wealth
   d. occupation and religion

5. A(n) _____ exists when the classes in a society are virtually closed. (p. 115)
   a. caste
   b. open class
   c. slave-state
   d. hierarchy

6. T F A caste member may switch classes through marriage. (p. 115)

7. T F Slaves are persons who do not own their labor, and as such represent a class. (p. 118)

8. T F In the Nupe system of Nigeria, a female slave could gain freedom through marriage. (p. 118)

9. T F According to Marshall Sahlins social stratification is the result of a society increasing its agricultural productivity. (p. 123)

10. T F Egalitarianism means that everyone is equal in a society. (p. 110)

WRITE ABOUT WHAT YOU HAVE READ

11. How do egalitarian, rank, and class societies vary in their access to economic resources, power, and prestige? Why?

12. What are the major differences between open class societies and caste societies?

13. Which industrialized countries have the most social mobility? The least? Can you suggest why?

14. What are the three major advantages that the caste system of India ensures those of the upper castes? How is slavery similar to a caste? How is it different?

15. What does Marshall Sahlins suggest to be the reason for the emergence of social stratification? How does he validate his view?

CHAPTER 8: *Sex, Gender, and Culture*

CHAPTER OUTLINE

I   Physique and Physiology

II Gender Roles
    A. Productive and Domestic Activities

III Relative Contributions to Subsistence

IV Political Leadership and Warfare

V   The Relative Status of Women

VI Personality Differences
    A. Misconceptions about Differences in Behavior

VII Sexuality
    A. Cultural Regulation of Sexuality: Permissiveness versus Restrictiveness
        1. Premarital Sex
        2. Extramarital Sex
        3. Sex in Marriage
        4. Homosexuality
        5. Reasons for Restrictiveness

MAJOR POINTS FOR REVIEW - CHAPTER SUMMARY

Chapter 8 takes on the huge task of dealing with the topics of sex, gender, and culture. The authors have divided this into two different topics: sex and gender differences and sexuality.

In the first portion they have divided the study further into a look at physique and physiology, gender roles, and personality. Their findings are interesting. Human males and females vary considerably in appearance even though many other animals do not. The explanation for this sexual dimorphism is not well understood. It could be that these gender differences are the result of both genetics and culture. Furthermore all societies prescribe certain tasks to men and women. This gender differentiation is usually explained by the physical size and strength differences between men and women. A further explanation of these gender patterns would include the compatibility of certain tasks with child rearing practices. Males can afford to be more mobile (e.g. hunting) as they do not have to breast-feed children.

Men contribute more to primary subsistence, in terms of calories, than women. Women however tend to contribute more time to the family if both primary and secondary subsistence patterns are counted together. Primary subsistence is the getting of food, while secondary subsistence is the preparation of food. Men typically are the political leaders and almost exclusively involved in warfare.

Further along the authors deal with the relative status of women. Status does not seem to carry over from one activity to another. In the absence of formal political systems, less complex societies have more opportunities for women to take status positions.

While Margaret Mead's research showed that the personality traits we call masculine and feminine are not linked to gender, newer studies disagree. In many cross-cultural surveys completed recently, it has been found that by as early an age as three to six, boys exhibit greater aggression than girls. Less well documented studies indicate that girls tend to be more nurturing and responsible.

Sexuality is the topic of the second half of the chapter. All societies have at least some rules for governing sexuality. The degree of permissiveness societies allow in sexual behavior is studied in premarital sex, extramarital sex, and sex within marriage. Societies that do not allow sexual expression between children also punish premarital and extramarital sex. Societies that are generally restrictive about heterosexuality are not necessarily restrictive about homosexuality. Societies that forbid abortion and infanticide for married women are likely to be intolerant of male homosexuality. Homosexuality and heterosexuality have to be considered separately when it comes to restrictiveness. This chapter provides many more examples of the restrictions that deal with both homosexuality and heterosexuality.

DEFINING THE GLOSSARY TERMS

Check your understanding of Chapter 8 by defining each of the glossary terms.

Compatibility-with-child-care theory

Economy-of-effort theory

Expendability theory

Gender differences

Gender roles

Gender stratification

Primary subsistence activities

Secondary subsistence activities

Sex differences

Sexually dimorphic

Strength theory

CHECK YOUR UNDERSTANDING

1. Refer to the *New Perspectives on Gender* box titled "Women's Electoral Success on the
   Northwest Coast.". What has Bruce Miller discovered about women's electoral success in
   Coast Salish communities? Why do they have such success? What do economics have to do
   with this? What does the size of the community have to do with women's success?

2. Refer to the *New Perspectives on Gender* box titled "Why Do Some Societies Allow Women to Participate in Combat?". What are the two factors that seem to be necessary to allow women to participate in combat? Would you expect the United States to eventually allow women to participate?

3. How are premarital and extramarital sex controlled in various societies? (e.g. What are the differences? Are there any differences due to degree of complexity? If so, what are they?)

TEST YOUR KNOWLEDGE

Select the best answer for the multiple choice questions and circle the letter T for true and F for false. Short answer essay questions should be answered in full sentences and as concisely as possible.

1. Males and females are demonstrably different in which of the following ways? (p. 127)
   a. Intelligence
   b. Percentage of fat for total body weight
   c. Ability to drive automobiles
   d. Ability to balance the family check book

2. Women in almost all societies are responsible for which task? (p. 128)
   a. Gathering of wild plants
   b. Hunting and trapping of animals
   c. Mining
   d. Production of musical instruments

3. The phrase secondary subsistence refers to (p. 130)
   a. the gathering of wild plants.
   b. the planting of food crops.
   c. the preparation and storage of foods.
   d. the preparation of sea foods.

4. Premarital sex is (p. 142)
   a. not allowed in societies that allow homosexuality.
   b. allowed in the same societies that allow homosexuality.
   c. more restricted in more complex societies.
   d. always allowed except in industrialized countries.

5. Homosexuality is (p. 141)
   a. always found at about the same levels in most societies.
   b. prohibited by almost all societies.
   c. practiced openly and encouraged in some societies.
   d. a very commonly used form of preparing men for marriage.

6. T F In most societies labor roles are fixed by gender. (p. 128)

7. T F If primary and secondary subsistence activities are counted together, then men work the
          most hours. (p. 130)

8. T F In almost all societies, men provide the most calories, because they do most of the
          gathering. (p. 130)

9. T F In about 85 percent of societies, men are the only political leaders. (p. 132)

10. T F The percentage of societies that allow women to participate in warfare is less than 20
          percent. (p. 132)

WRITE ABOUT WHAT YOU HAVE READ

11. How does the greater height of men relate to the fact that a much larger percentage of men
    are political leaders compared to women?

12. Use the following theories to explain gender roles? The strength theory, compatibility-with-child-theory, economy of effort theory, and the expendability theory.

13. How has the concept of the male bread-winner changed in our society? Why?

14. Describe the most common theory about why women have relatively high or low status. What affect upon women's status does warfare have? Why?

15. What gender differences in personality have been discovered recently? What has the Six Cultures Project demonstrated about personality?

CHAPTER 9: *Marriage and the Family*

CHAPTER OUTLINE

I   Marriage
   A. The Nayar "Exception"
   B. Rare Types of Marriage

II   Why is Marriage Universal?
   A. Gender Division of Labor
   B. Prolonged Infant Dependency
   C. Sexual Competition
   D. Other Mammals and Birds: Postpartum Requirements

III   How Does One Marry?
   A. Marking the Onset of Marriage
   B. Economic Aspects of Marriage
      1. Bride Price
      2. Bride Service
      3. Exchange of Females
      4. Gift Exchange
      5. Dowry
      6. Indirect Dowry

IV   Restrictions on Marriage: The Universal Incest Taboo
   A. Childhood-Familiarity Theory
   B. Freud's Psychoanalytic Theory
   C. Family-Disruption Theory
   D. Cooperation Theory
   E. Inbreeding Theory

V   Whom Should One Marry?
   A. Arranged Marriages
   B. Exogamy and Endogamy
   C. Cousin Marriages
   D. Levirate and Sororate

VI How Many Does One Marry?
   A. Polygyny
   B. Polyandry

VII The Family
   A. Variation in Family Form

B. Extended-Family Households
C. Possible Reasons for Extended-Family Households

MAJOR POINTS FOR REVIEW - CHAPTER SUMMARY

This chapter deals with a universal pattern in human societies: marriage. As defined in this book, marriage is a socially approved sexual and economic union that has reciprocal obligations between the two spouses and the spouses and their children. It is felt that, as marriage is universal, it must be adaptive. It is proposed that marriage solves several problems between males and females. The three major problems apparently solved by marriage are: gender division of labor, prolonged infant dependency and sexual competition between males for females.

Marriage may be universal but that does not mean every society deals with it in the same way. How people marry varies considerably, even as much as the economic considerations. In many societies (75%) some form of economic transaction must occur before the marriage can be formalized. These transactions include bride price, bride service, dowry, indirect dowry, gift exchange, or even the exchange of females.

The one marriage restriction that exists in all cultures is the incest taboo. Simply put it means that a person cannot marry particular kin members. The most universal aspect is the prohibition of sexual intercourse between parents and children and between siblings. Various theories exist as to why this prohibition is universal. Edward Westermarck proposed the childhood-familiarity theory; Sigmund Freud proposed that the incest taboo is a reaction against unconscious, unacceptable desires; and Bronislaw Malinowski hypothesized the family-disruption theory. The cooperation theory was first proposed by Edward Tylor, and then later elaborated by Claude Levi-Strauss and Leslie White. Probably the oldest idea that deals with the taboo of incest is the fear of inbreeding.

The next section of the chapter deals with the idea of who one marries. There are arranged marriages, levirate and sororate marriages, cousin marriages, and rules of exogamy and endogamy that force a person to marry outside of a predefined group or inside of a predefined group, respectively.

How many people one person can marry is also of some interest to anthropologists. In most societies the answer has been more than one. Monogamy (the marriage of one man to one woman) has actually been one of the least common practices between all societies. Most societies have allowed polygyny (the marriage of one man to more than one woman), while most have not allowed polyandry (the marriage of one woman to more than one man). Group marriage (where more than one man is married to more than one woman) is very uncommon.

Another cultural universal is the family. Families vary in structure from society to society. The most common form is the extended family. In this family, more than the mother, father and children (nuclear family) live in the same residence. It may include a married couple and their married children, or two married brothers and their entire families, including several generations of relatives. The smallest family, on the other hand, is the single-parent family, usually headed by the mother (matrifocal).

The question usually arises as to why the extended family is so popular? They are usually found in sedentary agricultural societies. The basic factor that makes them so common is economic in nature.

DEFINING THE GLOSSARY TERMS

Check your understanding of Chapter 9 by defining each of the glossary terms.

Berdaches

Bride price (or bride wealth)

Bride service

Cross-cousins

Dowry

Endogamy

Exogamy

Extended family

Family

Fraternal polyandry

Group marriage

Incest taboo

Indirect dowry

Levirate

Marriage

Matrifocal family

Monogamy

Nonfraternal polyandry

Nonsororal polygyny

Nuclear family

Parallel cousins

Polyandry

Polygamy

Polygyny

Postpartum sex taboo

Sororal polygyny

Sororate

CHECK YOUR UNDERSTANDING

1. Refer to the *Research Frontiers and Current Issues* box titled "The Husband-Wife Relationship: Variation in Love, Intimacy, and Sexual Jealousy." How do most societies view romantic love? What are the two conditions that predict the discouragement of love as a basis for marriage? How does intimacy compare to romantic love? Who are the most violent when it comes to sexual jealousy? Why?

2. What are the various types of marriage systems in relationship to how many people a person can marry? Define them. What are the advantages of each system of marriage? Why is it that in societies that allow polygyny, only a few percent of the males are in multiple marriages?

3. Refer to the *Research Frontiers and Current Issues* box titled "One-Parent Families: Why the Recent Increase?" What are the ways in which a one-parent family can be created? How is it that one-parent families survive in the United States and other countries without family support? How does employment affect the likelihood of women to marry?

TEST YOUR KNOWLEDGE

Select the best answer for the multiple choice questions and circle the letter T *for true and* F *for false. Short answer essay questions should be answered in full sentences and as concisely as possible*

1. Marriage is a socially approved _____ and _____ union between a male and female. (p. 145)
   a. sexual, parental
   b. economic, parental
   c. economic, intimate
   d. sexual, economic

2. Of the following, which is not a major reason for marriage? (p. 155)
   a. Gender division of labor
   b. Prolonged infant dependency
   c. Sexual competition
   d. Romantic love

3. _____ is a gift of money or goods from the groom or his kin to the bride's kin. (p. 149)
   a. Bride service
   b. Dowry
   c. Bride price
   d. Gift exchange

4. Sigmund Freud's psychoanalytic theory about the incest taboo is based upon the idea (p. 153)
   a. that people have an unconscious reaction against unacceptable desires.
   b. that sexual competition must be avoided between siblings.
   c. that brothers and sisters find each other boring.
   d. that inbreeding may be the result of incest.

5. _____ is the practice of marrying someone outside of the kin group or community. (p. 156)
   a. Endogamy
   b. Exogamy
   c. Polyandry
   d. Polygyny

6. T F Polyandry can be between a single woman and two or more men, or even a woman and a set of brothers. (p. 159)

7. T F The childhood-familiarity theory proposed by Carl Jung states that siblings are not attracted to each other since they have been closely associated with each other all of their early lives. (p. 152)

63

8. T F Bronislaw Malinowski, of Trobriand Island fame, states that sexual competition among family members would create so much rivalry and tension that the family could not function as an effective unit. (p. 153)

9. T F Arranged marriages were the norm in North America until the beginning of World War II. (p. 156)

10. T F The postpartum sex taboo practiced in tropical areas, may lead to the practice of polygyny and stave off a disease called marburg. (p. 159)

WRITE ABOUT WHAT YOU HAVE READ

11. What is marriage? Why the focus on both the sexual and economic aspects of it? What group did not practice marriage as all other societies do? Why?

12. How does marriage help in the sharing of the products of their labor? Why is marriage important to infants and children?

13. Compare bride price to the concept of the dowry.

14. Compare the family-disruption theory with the cooperation theory for an explanation of the incest taboo.

15. At what level is American society exogamous in its marriage practices? At what level are they endogamous? How have they changed over the last few decades?

CHAPTER 10: *Marital Residence and Kinship*

CHAPTER OUTLINE

I   Patterns of Marital Residence
   A. Patrilocal Residence
   B. Matrilocal Residence
   C. Bilocal Residence
   D. Avunculocal Residence
   E. Neolocal Residence

II   Explanations of Variation in Residence
   A. Neolocal Residence
   B. Matrilocal Versus Patrilocal Residence
   C. Bilocal Residence

III   The Structure of Kinship
   A. Rules of Descent
      1. Patrilineal Descent
      2. Matrilineal Descent
      3. Ambilineal Descent

IV   Bilateral Kinship

V   Unilineal Descent
   A. Types of Unilineal Descent Groups
      1. Lineages
      2. Clans
      3. Phratries
      4. Moieties
      5. Combinations
   B. Patrilineal Organization
   C. Matrilineal Organization
   D. Functions of Unilineal Descent Groups
      1. Regulating Marriage
      2. Economic Functions
      3. Political Functions
      4. Religious Functions
   E. Development of Unilineal Systems

VI   Ambilineal Systems

VII Kinship Terminology
   A. Inuit, or Eskimo, System
   B. Omaha System
   C. Crow System
   D. Iroquois System
   E. Sudanese System
   F. Hawaiian System

MAJOR POINTS FOR REVIEW - CHAPTER SUMMARY

Welcome to the chapter that deals with the true heart of social anthropology: marital residence and kinship. These are the bases for most other social relationships into which humans enter. Where people move when they marry (if they do at all), how they are related to other people, and how kinship is defined are the important components of this chapter.

It is here that we find some of the greatest variations in human social behavior. We take it for granted that our grandparents on both sides of our family are equivalent. Yet in some societies, not only would this not be the case, but one side or the other would not even be related. It happens also that a mother or father may not be a relative in some societies.

Marital residence is perhaps the simplest of these concepts to follow. There are five basic ways in which a newly married couple can be placed: patrilocal, matrilocal, bilocal, avunculocal, or even neolocal. The reasons for these arrangements are complex, and yet logical at the same time.

Kinship relationships are very important in noncommercial societies. These relationships may very well determine the access an individual has to various resources, or political alliances. Because of this, who your relatives are, is of greatest importance. Societies have developed rules of descent in order to help the individual. As a result each individual knows who to turn to in order to receive help. Societies that have descent rules with links of one sex only are unilineal (matrilineal and patrilineal). These groups can be further divided into various types such as lineages, clans, phratries, moieties, or even combinations of the four. Unilineal descent groups further function in the social arena by controlling whom one marries, defining political alliances, and may even determine specific religious beliefs and practices.

Kinship can also be bilateral or ambilineal. North Americans are the most familiar with bilateral kinship where both sides of the family are related to the individual. Kinship reckoning is horizontal. This system does not trace to a common ancestor. Ambilineal systems, on the other hand, are fairly rare. While this system is very similar to unilineal descent systems in many ways, it does vary in that an individual may be related through men or women. Some people in a society may be related through their fathers, while others are related through their mothers.

Finally, this chapter deals with how we classify our kin. Kinship terminology has long been confusing to students of anthropology for the simple reason that the variation in methods of naming relatives is great and quite different from our own. Two terms must be understood before anything else in this section makes sense: **consanguineal - relatives** related through blood, and **affinal - relatives** related through marriage. Six systems of identifying relatives (kin) exist throughout the world. These systems are related quite closely to types of descent groups. They either divide kin into quite complex webs of relationships (as in our own system) or they tend to lump many people into the same classification. In all systems however, it is the needs of society that have arranged these complex formulations.

DEFINING THE GLOSSARY TERMS

Check your understanding of Chapter 10 by defining each of the glossary terms.

Affinal kin

Ambilineal descent

Avunculocal residence

Bilateral kinship

Bilocal residence

Clan or sib

Classificatory term

Consanguineal kin

Descriptive term

Double descent or double unilineal descent

Ego

Kindred

Lineage

Matriclans

Matrilineage

Matrilineal descent

Matrilocal residence

Moiety

Neolocal residence

Patriclans

Patrilineage

Patrilineal descent

Patrilocal residence

Phratry

Rules of descent

Siblings

Totem

Unilineal descent

Unilocal residence

CHECK YOUR UNDERSTANDING

1. Refer to the *Current Research and Issues* box titled "Neolocality and Adolescent Rebellion:
   Are They Related?" Is adolescence experienced the same way in all societies? What type of
   residence pattern leads to independence? Why is conflict between parents and adolescents
   apparently absent in societies that practice forms of residence other than neolocal?

2. Review the box titled "The Main Predictors of Marital Residence Pattern" (Figure 10-2). What major factors lead to matrilocality? Patrilocality? What major economic factor leads to neolocality? Why?

3. Refer to the *New Perspectives on Gender* box titled "Variation in Residence and Kinship: What Difference does it Make to Women?" How does patrilineality and patrilocality detract from the status of women? Why? How is it that matrilineality and matrilocality may not add to the status of women? Why?

TEST YOUR KNOWLEDGE

Select the best answer for the multiple choice questions and circle the letter T *for true and* F *for false. Short answer essay questions should be answered in full sentences and as concisely as possible.*

1. _____ residence is when the daughter stays and the son leaves so that the married couple lives with or near the wife's parents. (p. 166)
   a. Patrilocal
   b. Matrilocal
   c. Bilocal
   d. Avunculocal

2. _____ residence is when both son and daughter normally leave, but the son and his wife settle with or near his mother's brother. (p. 166)
   a. Patrilocal
   b. Matrilocal
   c. Bilocal
   d. Avunculocal

3. In what type of society is neolocal residence common? (p. 167)
    a. Food collecting
    b. Horticultural
    c. Commercial
    d. Pastoral

4. Which is the most frequent rule of descent? (p. 171)
    a. Patrilineal
    b. Matrilineal
    c. Ambilineal
    d. Bilateral

5. A _____ is a set of kin whose members believe themselves to be descended from a common ancestor or ancestress, but the links back to that common ancestor are not specified. (p. 174)
    a. moiety
    b. lineage
    c. phratry
    d. clan

6. T F The matrilineal organization is the most common type of descent system. (p. 177)

7. T F Matrilineal organizations lead to much greater control of societies by females. (p. 176)

8. T F In unilineal societies, individuals are not usually permitted to marry within their own unilineal descent groups. (p. 178)

9. T F The Eskimo, or Inuit, kinship terminology system lumps cousins under the same term but distinguishes them from brothers and sisters. (p. 181)

10. T F The Sudanese system is the one system which lumps most relatives of the same generation under the same term. (p. 183)

WRITE ABOUT WHAT YOU HAVE READ

11. Compare the Omaha, Crow, and Iroquois kinship terminology systems.

12. Why does matrilineality not necessarily lead to increased political control by women?

13. Why are neolocal residence patterns so rare?

14. What features of patrilocality make it such a popular form of marital residence?

15. Describe ambilineal descent.

CHAPTER 11: *Associations and Interest Groups*

CHAPTER OUTLINE

I Nonvoluntary Associations
- A. Age-Sets
  - 1. Karimojong Age-Sets
  - 2. Shavante Age-Sets
- B. Unisex Associations
  - 1. Mae Enga Bachelor Associations
  - 2. Poro and Sande
  - 3. Ijaw Women's Associations

II Voluntary Associations
- A. Military Associations
- B. Regional Associations
- C. Ethnic Associations
- D. Rotating Credit Associations
- E. Multi-Ethnic Associations
- F. Other Interest Groups

III Explaining Variation in Associations

MAJOR POINTS FOR REVIEW - CHAPTER SUMMARY

Most people, somehow or other, belong to various associations or interest groups. This chapter describes the various types of associations and interest groups while showing the membership criteria and explaining the variation in associations. Associations are not based on kinship or territory. They do have several common characteristics, including some kind of formal, institutionalized structure, the ability to exclude some people, memberships of people with common interests or purposes, and pride in membership.

Two other criteria help determine membership: whether or not the association is voluntary and membership qualifications. Ethnic and regional are generally voluntary. An example of involuntary association would be the old for of the draft in the United States military. Membership qualifications can be divided into qualities that are achieved or ascribed. Achieved qualities are those which a person acquires throughout life, whereas ascribed qualities are those with which a person is born (gender, social class, etc.). Furthermore, ascribed qualities can be variable, in other words, some qualities are only found in some societies (religious, ethnic, or social class differences).

Probably the most involuntary organizations would be the age-grade and the age-set. These are composed of groups of people who belong to the same age or age and sex grouping. Movement through society would be inside of one of these groups. In industrialized societies, associations tend to be based on achieved qualities of the members, replacing the variably ascribed qualities found in members of associations in non-industrialized societies. These groups would be the most voluntary.

DEFINING THE GLOSSARY TERMS

Check your understanding of Chapter 11 by defining each of the glossary terms.

Achieved qualities

Age-grade

Age-set

Ascribed qualities

Associations

Unisex association

Universally ascribed qualities

Variably ascribed qualities

CHECK YOUR UNDERSTANDING

1. Refer to the *New Perspectives on Gender* box titled "Do Separate Women's Associations Increase Women's Status and Power?" What are the four aspects of women's political participation reviewed by Marc Howard Ross? What effect, upon the power women control, do women's associations have? Can separate science and math classes for females have an effect upon learning? How?

2. Refer to the *Current Research and Issues* box titled "Why do Street Gangs Develop, and Why are they Violent?" Who joins street gangs? What is the form of the Mexican-American street gang initiation? Why? What family stresses may lead to street gang membership?

3. What is S. N. Eisenstadt's hypothesis about age-sets? How could this be related to adolescent street gangs in our own society?

TEST YOUR KNOWLEDGE

Select the best answer for the multiple choice questions and circle the letter T for true and F for false. Short answer essay questions should be answered in full sentences and as concisely as possible.

1. Age, as a membership qualification for an age-set is a(n) (p. 187)
    a. achieved quality.
    b. ascribed quality.
    c. universally ascribed quality.
    d. variably ascribed quality.

2. The Karimojong age-set comprises all the men who have been initiated into manhood within a span of about five or six years. These age-sets are combined into (p. 188)
    a. generation sets.
    b. gender sets.
    c. professional associations.
    d. herding associations.

3. The Shavante male age-set functions to (p. 189)
    a. give boys a period of leisure-time before adulthood.
    b. train boys in the ways of hunting, weapon making, and ceremonial skills.
    c. train shaman in the careful maintenance of health in their society.
    d. teach boys how to be proper horticulturalists.

4. What is the major purpose of a male unisex association? (p. 189)
    a. To teach men how to play their proper role in society
    b. To teach boys how to play their proper role in society
    c. To strengthen the concept of male superiority and to offer men refuge from females
    d. To provide dramatic male initiations to all males in the society

5. S. N. Eisenstadt studied African age-sets and found that (p. 199)
    a. age-set systems fill the void that kinship groups leave when they fail to carry out functions necessary to the integration of society.
    b. age-set systems meet the needs of male or female solidarity.
    c. age-set systems provide the necessary leisure-time activities necessary for most people.
    d. age-grade systems bring about unity between males and females of a society.

6. T F One function of the serrano regional association, in Lima, Peru, is to acculturate newly arrived serranos to the urban life of Lima. (p. 195)

7. T F Regional associations maintain the same set of functions through time. (p. 195)

8. T F A tribal union in western Africa may function to keep traditions alive. (p. 195)

77

9. T F A person who joins a rotating credit association must fill out paperwork just like at a bank. (p. 197)

10. T F A superior skill, such as being a good airplane pilot, would be classified as a variably ascribed quality. (p. 187)

WRITE ABOUT WHAT YOU HAVE READ

11. During most of the Vietnam War, the United States Army drafted many of its members. Today, the draft does not exist (registration does not equal draft). What are the membership criteria for today's military and what kind of association has it become?

12. Describe the Karimojong age system. Which group plays the most authoritative role? Why?

13. Describe the various functions of the Ijaw Women's Associations.

14. How have modern Lakota military associations adapted to the outside world?

15. How do the large number of Norwegian clubs relate to the low crime rate?

CHAPTER 12: *Political Life: Social Order and Disorder*

CHAPTER OUTLINE

I Variation in Types of Political Organization
   A. Band Organization
   B. Tribal Organization
      1. Kinship Bonds
      2. Age-Set Systems
   C. Chiefdom Organization
   D. State Organization
   E. Factors Associated with Variation in Political Organization

II The Spread of State Societies

III Variation in Political Process
   A. Getting to Be a Leader
      1. "Big Men"
      2. "Big Women"
   B. Political Participation

IV Resolution of Conflict
   A. Peaceful Resolution of Conflict
      1. Avoidance
      2. Community Action
      3. Negotiation and Mediation
      4. Ritual Reconciliation - Apology
      5. Oaths and Ordeals
      6. Adjudication, Courts, and Codified Law
   B. Violent Resolution of Conflict
      1. Individual Violence
      2. Feuding
      3. Raiding
      4. Large-Scale Confrontations
   C. Explaining Warfare

MAJOR POINTS FOR REVIEW - CHAPTER SUMMARY

From the simplest to the most complex, all societies have some form of political system. The level of political integration inside a society can range from extremely informal to very formal political mechanisms. Elman Service suggested four levels of political integration: bands, tribes, chiefdoms, and states. Bands exist mainly in small societies where the people are nomadic. The nomadic group is the largest political unit. Tribal organization is not much more organized. It is multilocal and seemingly fragile. The integration of several villages may occur only under threat from the outside. Tribes would therefore make a much more potent military force than a band. In both cases, bands and tribes are mostly egalitarian. It is generally kinship bonds that bring together the various communities into tribes. Chiefdoms have formal mechanisms for integrating more than one community into a political unit. A chiefdom is generally headed by a chief who outranks all others. Populations tend to be dense and the communities are permanent. State level organization is the most complex and has the most formal integration mechanisms. Modern nations are all examples of state-level societies. A simple definition given in this text is that the state is "an autonomous political unit, encompassing many communities within its territory and having a centralized government with the power to collect taxes, draft men for work or war, and decree and enforce laws." States can use legitimate force to implement policies both internally and externally.

The next section of this chapter deals with a less understood process. Who gets power? In some societies heredity plays the leading role. "Big Men" and "Big Women" gain positions of prestige in otherwise egalitarian societies, through competition. Political participation in societies varies enormously. The degree of political participation seems to be high in small-scale societies, as well as in modern democratic states. Another interesting point is that democratically governed states do not go to war with each other.

Conflicts between groups can be resolved peacefully or violently. The peaceful route has the most variation. Societies can turn to avoidance as a means of shunning violence. Community action, negotiation and mediation, ritual reconciliation, oaths and ordeals, and more formal mechanisms such as adjudication, involving the use of courts and laws are all peaceful. Violent conflicts tend to occur when one or more of these techniques fail. Violence can take form on the individual level; can become feuding, raiding, or even warfare. Warfare, or large-scale conflict, only takes place in groups that practice intensive agriculture or industrialization.

DEFINING THE GLOSSARY TERMS

Check your understanding of Chapter 12 by defining each of the glossary terms.

Adjudication

Band

Band Organization

Chief

Chiefdom

Codified laws

Complementary opposition

Crime

Feuding

Headman

Mediation

Negotation

Oath

Ordeal

Raiding

Segmentary lineage system

State

State organization

Tribal organization

Tribe

Warfare

CHECK YOUR UNDERSTANDING

1. Refer to the *Current Research Issues* box titled "Democracy and Economic Development: How and Why are They Related?" Why is democracy associated with economic development? How do the cross-national and cross-cultural surveys contradict each other? How can this be reconciled?

2. Refer to the *New Perspectives on Gender* box titled "New Courts Allow Women to Address Grievances in Papua New Guinea," Describe Village Courts. How do women use these to redress serious charges against men? How has this system led to some equivalency in relations between men and women in Papuan society?

3. Refer to the Table 12-1 "Suggested Trends in Political Organization…" How do social differentiation and the major form of distribution compare to the type of organization? What does population density have to do with this relationship?

TEST YOUR KNOWLEDGE

Select the best answer for the multiple choice questions and circle the letter T *for true and* F *for false. Short answer essay questions should be answered in full sentences and as concisely as possible.*

1. A _____ is generally the head of a band. (p. 203)
   a. drummer
   b. chief
   c. headman
   d. minister

2. Bands and tribes have what type of social differentiation? (p. 204)
   a. Egalitarian
   b. Rank
   c. Class
   d. Caste

3. A chiefdom has some _____ structure that integrates more than one community into a political unit. (p. 206)
   a. informal
   b. legal
   c. formal
   d. customary

4. The power of mana in _____ chiefs was such that only after a chief had been converted to Christianity could the populace be converted. (p. 206)
   a. Asian
   b. African
   c. South African
   d. Polynesian

5. A _____ is an autonomous political unit, encompassing many communities within its territory and having a centralized government with the power to collect taxes, draft men for work, or war, and decree and enforce laws. (p. 206)
   a. country
   b. state
   c. chiefdom
   d. tribe

6. T F Multi-ethnic or multisociety states may form voluntarily, as in the case of Switzerland. (p. 207)

7. T F Societies with higher levels of political integration are more likely to exhibit social differentiation, especially in the form of class distinctions. (p. 209)

8. T F Smallpox, measles, and the other former scourges of Europe had largely become childhood diseases that most individuals of European ancestry survived. (p. 209)

9. T F The world will definitely be politically unified by the twenty-third century. (p. 210)

10. T F One form of conflict resolution is avoidance. (p. 214)

WRITE ABOUT WHAT YOU HAVE READ

11. List and describe the six means of conflict resolution. Which method is most useful in the resolution of conflicts inside the family? Why?

12. What is feuding? What is its apparent function?

13. Why do preindustrial peoples go to war? What effect do formal alliances between nations have on the frequency of warfare? Why?

14. Describe the coercive power, or lack thereof, of the band, tribe, chiefdom, and state.

15. How does a person become a chief in a chiefdom? How does a chief exercise power?

CHAPTER 13: *Psychology and Culture*

CHAPTER OUTLINE

I   The Universality of Psychological Development
    A. Early Research on Emotional Development
    B. Research on Cognitive Development

II Cross-Cultural Variation in Psychological Characteristics
    A. Child-Rearing Explanations
        1. Parental Acceptance and Rejection
        2. Task Assignment
        3. Schooling
    B. General Cultural Themes as Explanations
        1. Concepts of the Self
    C. Adaptational Explanations
    D. Possible Genetic and Physiological Influences
    E. Mental Illness

III Psychological Explanations of Cultural Variation

MAJOR POINTS FOR REVIEW - CHAPTER SUMMARY

This chapter deals with the psychological development of individuals inside of their societies; the influence culture has on their development, how psychological characteristics vary cross-culturally; and various explanations for cultural variation due to psychological variation.

The authors begin by investigating the universality of psychological development. A review of early research on both emotional and cognitive development is presented. Malinowski and Mead both questioned many of the earlier, Western theories that all children go through similar stages of emotional development. A theory of cognitive development, developed by Jean Piaget, is utilized in this chapter to question the results of many tests given to individuals of non-Western societies.

Cross-cultural variation in psychological characteristics is also discussed in this chapter. Child-rearing practices are reviewed cross-culturally- such as how often babies are held, whether children are encouraged to be aggressive, task assignment, and whether or not children attend formal schools. Socialization practices between societies are studied, specifically how well children conform to the training given to them by the society and parents. Mental illness is viewed in a cross-cultural framework- some illnesses are apparently universal, while others are not. It is demonstrated that much variation exists between societies in the area of personality.

Finally, explanation for these variations in personality is explored. In this review, cultural variation between societies is seen as a reflection of psychological variation. One example is developed by David McClelland. His research suggests that societies that develop high levels of achievement motivation in individuals will be likely to experience high rates of economic growth. So this chapter basically goes full-circle, from how cultural variation leads to psychological variation, to how psychological variation leads to a variation in cultural traits.

DEFINING THE GLOSSARY TERMS

Check your understanding of Chapter13 by defining each of the glossary terms.

Personality

Personality integration of culture

Primary institutions

Projective tests

Secondary institutions

Socialization (or enculturation)

CHECK YOUR UNDERSTANDING

1. Refer to the *Current Research Issues* box titled "Do Schools Teach Values?" What are the values taught in Chinese, Japanese, and United States preschools? How are values taught in each society?

2. Refer to the *New Perspectives on Gender* box titled "Do Women have a Different Morality?" What is the proposal by Carol Gilligan? What is the evidence for her proposal? What evidence contradicts it?

3. What types of mental illnesses are specific to particular cultures? How does anorexia nervosa fit this pattern? What types of mental illnesses are seemingly universal? Why?

TEST YOUR KNOWLEDGE

Select the best answer for the multiple choice questions and circle the letter T *for true and* F *for false. Short answer essay questions should be answered in full sentences and as concisely as possible.*

1. Abram Kardiner originally suggested that _____ patterns influence personality development through child training and that the resulting personality characteristics in turn influence the _____. (p. 238)
   a. cultural, culture
   b. maternity, culture
   c. parental, culture
   d. parental, society

2. David McClelland's research suggests that societies that develop high levels of achievement motivation in individuals will be likely to experience high rates of (p. 238)
   a. mental illness.
   b. educated individuals.
   c. economic growth.
   d. psychological conflicts.

3. Some anthropologists believe that child-rearing practices are largely _____ and that a society produces the kinds of personalities best suited to performance of the activities of the society. (p. 234)
   a. cultural
   b. psychological
   c. experimental
   d. adaptive

4. _____ is a term used by anthropologists and psychologists to describe the development, through the influence of parents and other people, of patterns of behavior in children that conform to cultural expectations. (p. 228)
   a. Acculturation
   b. Enculturation
   c. Socialization
   d. Motivation

5. Margaret Mead studied (p. 223)
   a. adolescence in Samoa.
   b. psychological development in southern Africa.
   c. aggression in the Yanamamo of Venezuela.
   d. adolescent behavior in the Trobriand Islands.

6. T F Bronislaw Malinowski questioned the universality of the Oedipus complex. (p. 224)

7. T F It is a tenant of Jean Piaget's theory of cognitive development that the development of thinking occurs in a series of stages. (p. 224-225)

8. T F A study of unconventional families in California showed that unconventional families held their children much more than more conventional families. (p. 226)

9. T F In Yanamamo families, children are punished for striking each other or their parents. (p. 227)

10. T F Games of strategy are associated with child training that emphasizes obedience. (p. 239)

WRITE ABOUT WHAT YOU HAVE READ

11. Describe the three major socialization influences on children. What are their functions?

12. What did psychologist Otto Klineberg mean when he said "How could psychologists speak of human attributes and human behavior when they knew only one kind of human beings?"

13. What are the concepts of conservation and reversibility described by Piaget?

14. Why do the Yanamamo raise their children to be so aggressive? Why are North American children not trained to be so aggressive?

15. How do TAT tests work and what is it that they reveal about the personality of the person taking the test?

CHAPTER 14: *Religion and Magic*

CHAPTER OUTLINE

I   The Universality of Religion
    A. The Need to Understand
    B. Reversions to Childhood Feelings
    C. Anxiety and Uncertainty
    D. The Need for Community

II Variation in Religious Beliefs
    A. Types of Supernatural Forces and Beings
        1. Supernatural Forces
        2. Supernatural Beings
    B. The Character of Supernatural Beings
    C. Structure or Hierarchy of Supernatural Beings
    D. Intervention of the Gods in Human Affairs
    E. Life after Death

III Variation in Religious Practices
    A. Ways to Interact with the Supernatural
    B. Magic
        1. Sorcery and Witchcraft
    C. Types of Practitioners
        1. The Shaman
        2. Sorcerers and Witches
        3. Mediums
        4. Priests
        5. Practitioners and Social Complexity

IV Religion and Adaptation
    A. Religious Change as Revitalization
        1. The Seneca and the Religion of Handsome Lake
        2. Cargo Cults

MAJOR POINTS FOR REVIEW - CHAPTER SUMMARY

Religion is another of the universal cultural characteristics which anthropologists study. The practice of religion apparently dates back at least 60,000 years and is found in every culture ever studied, past or present. While the discipline of anthropology is not interested in which religion is the best, it is interested in why its practice is universal. Five major theories have been proposed. Edward Tylor proposed that people simply needed to understand such things as dreams, trances, and death. Sigmund Freud believed that religion was an outgrowth of guilt and remorse of sons for killing their fathers. Bronislaw Malinowski later hypothesized that religion stemmed from major anxieties, especially about death itself, while Carl Jung felt that religion could act as a therapeutic aid in maturation. Emile Durkheim felt that religion originated with the society and not the individual. He felt that religion symbolized the society, so that it was the society itself that was being worshipped. In this way people met their need for community.

Religion and religious beliefs come in various forms. Supernatural forces do not have personalities. Mana and taboo, the forces for good and evil, are examples. Supernatural beings can be divided into gods and spirits. Gods are named and are usually made in the form of humans. They can exist alone, and be supreme, as in monotheism, or they can exist in a panoply of types, as in polytheistic religions, where no one god dominates. Spirits are unnamed. Some may be guardians and others could be hobgoblins. Ghosts and ancestor spirits form a class of beings who were once human. The gods are famous for being able to intervene in human affairs. Clifford Geertz makes the point that people explain unusual events through the intervention of the gods. Finally, the concept of life after death is quite common among religions. The variation between them is very interesting.

How interaction occurs between people and the supernatural is of great interest to anthropologists. This chapter looks cross-culturally at this and shows that some societies pray quietly, while others do so loudly. Prayer can be spontaneous or memorized. Some groups use hallucinogenic drugs, alcohol, sensory deprivation, exhaustion, or even repetitive drumming. These practices tend to be used to induce trance. Simulation and divination may be used to ask for guidance from the supernatural. Unlike prayers, which are requests, magic is the act of compelling the supernatural to work in your favor. Magic comes in two basic forms: witchcraft and sorcery. The former is performed through mental or emotional means, while the latter is practiced using material objects. An accusation of witchcraft cannot be proven or disproved as there is never any evidence. Other practitioners of the supernatural world include shamans, usually a part-time male specialist of high status; mediums, females who act on a part-time basis to heal while in a trance; and priests, usually full-time male specialists who are able to relate to gods which are beyond the reach of an ordinary person's control.

The final section of this chapter deals with religion as an adaptive force in society. All religions are argued to be adaptive because they reduce the anxieties and uncertainties that affect all people. Religious change, especially the founding of new religions, is fairly common in areas where some large-scale social changes have occurred. For example, contact with dominant societies, such as that between Europeans and Native American groups in North America have led to several revitalization movements. This chapter exemplifies the Seneca of New York, and Melanesian Cargo Cults.

DEFINING THE GLOSSARY TERMS

Check your understanding of Chapter 14 by defining each of the glossary terms.

Ancestor spirits

Animatism

Animism

Divination

Ghosts

Gods

Magic

Mana

Mediums

Monotheistic

Polytheistic

Priests

Religion

Revitalization movements

Shaman

Sorcery

Spirits

Supernatural

Taboo

Witchcraft

CHECK YOUR UNDERSTANDING

1. Refer to the *Current Research and Issues* box titled "The Usefulness of Religion: Taboos among New England Fishermen." How can taboos reduce anxiety? What did John Poggie and Richard Pollnac discover about taboos of New England fishermen and the distance of the fishing trip? What do the fishermen call their taboos? Do they believe in them? Do you believe the fishermen believe in them?

2. What are the major similarities and differences between monotheism, polytheism, and animism?

3. Refer to the *Current Issues* box titled "One Appeal of Religion May Be the Wish for a Better World." Why are the Protestant churches named Protestant? Who were the Pilgrims? What is the *millennium* in religious terms?

TEST YOUR KNOWLEDGE

Select the best answer for the multiple choice questions and circle the letter T *for true and* F *for false. Short answer essay questions should be answered in full sentences and as concisely as possible.*

1. Religion is any set of attitudes, beliefs, and practices pertaining to _____. (p. 242)
   a. god
   b. spirits
   c. supernatural power
   d. perceived power

2. Herodotus, in the fifth century B.C., noticed evidence for _____ of religious practices in the fifty societies that he visited. (p. 242)
   a. diffusion
   b. similarities
   c. independent invention
   d. large differences

3. Carl Jung suggested that religion (p. 243)
   a. is a useful intercession between us and the gods.
   b. is not just a way of dealing with anxiety, it is thought to be therapeutic.
   c. causes us to symbolize society.
   d. reduces our anxieties, especially those about death.

4. _____ is what R. R. Marett calls religious beliefs which have no personalities. (p. 243)
   a. Animism
   b. Secularism
   c. Polytheism
   d. Animatism

5. _____ is the act of compelling supernatural beings to act in some particular and intended way. (p. 249)
   a. Prayer
   b. Magic
   c. Voodoo
   d. Hoodoo

6. T F Witchcraft is impossible to prove because evidence of witchcraft can never be found. (p. 249)

7. T F A shaman is a practitioner of evil who uses articles or objects. (p. 250-251)

8. T F The Seneca revitalization movement, called the ghost dance, had five main sections: temperance, peace and social unity, preservation of tribal lands, proacculturation, and domestic morality. (p. 253-254)

9. T F Cargo cults originated on Buka in the Solomon Islands. The leaders prophesied that a tidal wave would sweep away the villages and a ship would arrive with iron, axes, food, tobacco, cars, and arms. (p. 254-255)

10. T F Clifford Geertz contends that when faced with ignorance, pain, and the unjustness of life that a person explains events by the intervention of the gods. (p. 247)

WRITE ABOUT WHAT YOU HAVE READ

11. Why arc supernatural forces and natural forces impossible to compare?

12. Describe the various types of supernatural beings. What are their functions?

13. What does Swanson suggest is the reason for societies having a high god?

14. Compare magic with prayer.

15. What are simulation and divination? How do people in American society practice
    divination? Why do the Naskapi consult a diviner?

CHAPTER 15: *The Arts*

CHAPTER OUTLINE

I   Body Decoration and Adornment

II   Explaining Variation in the Arts
  A. Visual Art
  B. Music
  C. Folklore

III   Viewing the Art of Other Cultures

IV   Artistic Change and Culture Contact

MAJOR POINTS FOR REVIEW - CHAPTER SUMMARY

The majority of societies have not practiced art for art's sake. Art in most societies has been incorporated into other practices such as religion, and social and political life. Even so, art is defined here as having several qualities: it expresses as well as communicates; it stimulates the senses, affects emotions, and evokes ideas; it is produced in culturally patterned ways and styles; and it has cultural meaning. Some people are said to be better at it than others. One thing is definite: there is a huge amount of variation in how it is produced and even what is called art.

Body decoration is one art form that is practiced in many societies. It can take the form of tattooing, scarring, or changes in shape. Body decoration can be used to delineate social status, sex, occupation, local and ethnic identity, or religion within a society. Body adornment can also take on sexual connotations in its erotic significance.

Art varies tremendously from society to society. Art can take on various forms in the style of visual, music, dance, and folklore. Some interesting conclusions are presented in this chapter. For example, John Fischer notes that egalitarian artists tend to use empty space as a design element, while in more complex societies, artwork is more crowded. In music, it has been found that polyphony is related to a high degree of female participation in food getting. Modern folklore (urban legends) is seen as having the same meaning as myths of the past did in earlier societies. Societies that are nomadic have been found to have portable art, such as song, dance, and folklore, while specialized artists are only found in societies with a complex and specialized division of labor.

Art has changed rapidly as many indigenous peoples have lost their cultures. Many artistic traditions have been lost or transformed for commercial sale. Just the same, art is expressed by all in some form or other.

DEFINING THE GLOSSARY TERMS

Check your understanding of Chapter 15 by defining each of the glossary terms.

Folklore

Polyphony

CHECK YOUR UNDERSTANDING

1. Refer to the *Current Research and Issues* box titled "Politics and Art." Why do Melanesian leaders paint their bodies while Polynesian leaders tattoo theirs? How do Samoan tattoos indicate social status? What are Lewis Austin's conclusions about a person's political ideology?

2. Refer to the *Current Research and Issues* box titled "Do Masks Show Emotion in Universal Ways?" How does emotion, as displayed by the face, vary from culture to culture? Why? How does this relate to masks used by various cultures?

3. List the five themes recurrent in myths as noted by Clyde Kluckhohn. What pattern do hero myths follow, according to Edward Tylor? According to Joseph Campbell, hero myths resemble initiations. How? Why can a satisfactory conclusion about myths be reached at this time?

TEST YOUR KNOWLEDGE

Select the best answer for the multiple choice questions and circle the letter T *for true and* F *for false. Short answer essay questions should be answered in full sentences and as concisely as possible.*

1. Art is everything listed below except for which of the following. (p. 258)
   a. Indifferent
   b. Evocative
   c. Emotional
   d. Representational

2. The tendency to decorate the body is probably _____. (p. 258)
   a. stupid
   b. infantile
   c. lower class
   d. universal

3. _____ anthropologists feel that art expresses the typical feelings, anxieties, and experiences of people in a culture. (p. 259)
   a. Medical
   b. Social
   c. Psychological
   d. Applied

4. It has been discovered that polyphony in music is related to (p. 264)
   a. a high degree of male hunting behavior.
   b. a high degree of female hunting behavior.
   c. a low degree of food intake by a hunter-gatherer group.
   d. a high degree of female participation in food-getting.

5. Which is not one of the five themes, found in myths, as listed by Clyde Kluckhohn?
    (p. 268)
    a. the slaying of monsters
    b. catastrophe
    c. sibling rivalry
    d. food shortages

6. T F Unprovoked aggression is likely in folktales of societies that are subject to
        unpredictable food shortages. (p. 269)

7. T F The Navajo probably borrowed weaving skills from the Hopi. (p. 270)

8. T F There is some evidence that the symbolism used in masks is often universal.
        (p. 264)

9. T F Tattooing is always used to display rank in non-Western societies. (p. 258)

10. T F Alan Lomax found that song style varied with cultural complexity. The more culturally
        complex a society, the more nonsense words are used in a song. (p. 263)

WRITE ABOUT WHAT YOU HAVE READ

11. How does music vary due to cultural complexity? Compare that to the findings by John
    Fischer on art.

12. What are the two major function of masks?

13. Compare the views on mythology by Clyde Kluckhohn, Edward Tylor, and Joseph Campbell.

14. What are urban legends? What function do they play in modern society?

15. How does cultural contact change the artistic practices of a society?

CHAPTER 16: *Culture Change and Globalization*

CHAPTER OUTLINE

I   How and Why Cultures Change
    A. Discovery and Invention
        1. Unconscious Invention
        2. Intentional Innovation
        3. Who Adopts Innovations?
        4. Costs and Benefits
    B. Diffusion
        1. Patterns of Diffusion
        2. The Selective Nature of Diffusion
    C. Acculturation
    D. Revolution

II Culture Change and Adaptation

III Types of Culture Change in the Modern World
    A. Commercialization
        1. Migratory Labor
        2. Nonagricultural Commercial Production
        3. Supplementary Cash Crops
        4. Introduction of Commercial and Industrial Agriculture
    B. Religious Change
        1. Christianity on Tikopia
    C. Political and Social Change

IV Globalization: Problems and Opportunities

V   Ethnogenesis: The Emergence of New Cultures

VI Cultural Diversity in the Future

MAJOR POINTS FOR REVIEW - CHAPTER SUMMARY

The subject of this chapter is probably the major focus of anthropology today: how and why cultures change. Three questions are presented here about culture change: 1. What is the source of a new trait? 2. Why are people motivated to adopt it? 3. Is the new trait adaptive?

Change is affected in several ways. This chapter explores the mechanisms of discovery and invention, unconscious invention (accidental juxtaposition), intentional innovation, and who adopts inventions. Diffusion is also explored as a means of culture change. There are three patterns of diffusion: direct contact, intermediate contact, and stimulus. Direct contact refers to contact between two groups. The neighboring group adopts an idea or invention. Intermediate contact requires a third party such as a trader. An idea or invention is carried from one group to another. Stimulus diffusion is quite different. Just the knowledge of an idea may stimulate a group to invent something similar. One last type of diffusion, acculturation, refers to the borrowing of cultural traits under external pressure.

Cultural traits act much like biologically inherited traits. If they are adaptive, or at least not maladaptive, they will stay an essential element of the society. In fact, adaptive traits should increase in frequency in a society through time, while maladaptive traits should dwindle away. Of course, changes in the environment, both social and physical, can make formerly adaptive traits maladaptive and maladaptive traits adaptive.

The next section of this chapter deals with the direction culture change has taken since A.D. 1500. Since then the expansion of Western societies has induced culture change, in some cases forcefully, upon nearly the rest of the world. Japan and China have also been responsible for stimulating culture change. One of the largest changes due to the expansion of Western societies is commercialization. Most societies had never used money or grew crops for cash. As commercialization takes hold in a society, the entire economic base is changed, along with an accompanying alteration in social, political, and even psychological elements of the society.

Globalization is now being studied by anthropologists, all over the world. Its affects are numerous and the fears of it extinguishing cultural systems are rampant. Actually, the world has been undergoing globalization for centuries. Clearly the world is no longer regionalized as it was before colonialism. Globalization is of concern because it is grander than all of the other diffusion processes of the past. As societies become more and more interdependent cultural diversity is minimized, but it is not eliminated.

Finally, culture change brings us ethnogenesis; the creation of new cultures. During the many diffusion processes of the past, many groups have been displaced, forming new cultures. Today, many new cultures exist with shared religions, languages, and a common origin.

DEFINING THE GLOSSARY TERMS

Check your understanding of Chapter 16 by defining each of the glossary terms.

Acculturation

Diffusion

Ethnogenesis

Globalization

Peasants

Revolution

CHECK YOUR UNDERSTANDING

1. Refer to the *Applied Anthropology* box titled "Obesity, Hypertension, and Diabetes: Health Consequences of Modernization?" What are the two consequences of modern medical care? What health problems occur due, in part, to old age? What patterns have become clear in researching Samoans of both urban and rural backgrounds? Are disease processes cultural, natural, or both? Explain your answer.

2. Refer to the *Current Research and Issues* box titled "Culture Change and Persistence in Communist China." How did government health policies lead to greater family ties? What is the experience of Han Chinese who moved into Inner Mongolia? Why do pastoralist children tend to stay in school longer than farming children? What does the expression "we hide from our cousins but not our friends," mean?

3. What has been the downfall of authoritarian governments throughout the world?

TEST YOUR KNOWLEDGE

Select the best answer for the multiple choice questions and circle the letter T *for true and* F *for false. Short answer essay questions should be answered in full sentences and as concisely as possible.*

1. Tikopia, a Polynesian island, was one of the few to retain its traditional religion until this century. Almost all Tikopians changed to Christianity mostly because of a(n) _____ in 1955, which killed the three major non-Christian leaders. (p. 287)
    a. war
    b. epidemic
    c. invasion
    d. famine

2. It is the process of _____ which is the consequence of dozens of tiny initiatives, according to Ralph Linton. (p. 274)
    a. diffusion
    b. stimulus diffusion
    c. invention
    d. unconscious invention

3. Who, in a society, tends to adopt new inventions early? (p. 275)
    a. The less well off
    b. Those who need them the most
    c. Educated, upwardly mobile individuals
    d. Everyone tends to adopt at the same time

4. What type of diffusion occurs when two neighboring groups share an invention?
   (p. 276)
   a. Direct contact
   b. Stimulus
   c. Intermediate diffusion
   d. Hierarchical diffusion

5. One of the most important changes resulting from the expansion of Western societies is the increasingly worldwide dependence on? (p. 282)
   a. Labor economy
   b. Communism
   c. Socialism
   d. Commercial exchange

6. T F Commercialization in Tikopia has led to stronger kinship ties. (p. 283)

7. T F Peasants are rural people who produce food for others, such as a landlord. (p. 285)

8. T F The changeover to commercial agriculture may result in an improved standard of living in the short and long run. (p. 285)

9. T F Western missionaries have brought about prosperity wherever they have gone. (p. 286)

10. T F Globalization refers to the massive flow of goods, people, information, and capitol across huge areas of the earth's surface is . (p. 288)

11. T F In some ways, globalization is causing cultural changes in similar directions. (p. 288)

WRITE ABOUT WHAT YOU HAVE READ

12. How do discovery and invention differ from each other?

13. Why is it that well educated, upwardly mobile people adopt new ideas and inventions more quickly than the people who need them the most?

14. Compare direct contact diffusion, intermediate contact diffusion, and stimulus diffusion.

15. What is acculturation? How did the Spanish practice it in their conquest of Mexico over four hundred years ago?

16. Describe and explain the four conditions that may exist to give rise to rebellion?

CHAPTER 17: *Applied and Practicing Anthropology*

CHAPTER OUTLINE

I   Motives for Applying and Practicing Anthropology

II   History and Types of Application

III Ethics of Applied Anthropology

IV Evaluating the Effects of Planned Change

V Difficulties in Instituting Planned Change
    A. Resistance by the Target Population
    B. Discovering and Utilizing Local Channels of Influence
    C. Need for More Collaborative Applied Anthropology

VI Cultural Resource Management

VII Forensic Anthropology

MAJOR POINTS FOR REVIEW - CHAPTER SUMMARY

Applied anthropology in the United States developed out of anthropologists' personal experiences with disadvantaged peoples. Applied, or practicing, anthropologists may be involved in one or more phases of a program that is designed to change peoples' lives: assembling relevant knowledge, constructing alternative plans, assessing the likely social and environmental impact of particular plans, implementing the program, and monitoring the program and its effects.

Today, many anthropologists are finding employment outside of anthropology departments - in medical schools, health centers, development agencies, urban-planning agencies, and other public and private organizations.

The code of ethics for those who work professionally as applied anthropologists, specifies that the target population should be included as much as possible in the formulation of policy, so that people in the community may know in advance how the program may affect them. But perhaps the most important aspect of the code is the pledge not to be involved in any plan whose effect will not be beneficial. It is often difficult to evaluate the effects of planned changes. Long-term consequences may be detrimental even if the changes are beneficial in the short run.

Even if a planned change will prove beneficial to its target population, the people may not accept it. And if the proposed innovation is not utilized by the intended target, the project cannot be considered a success. Target populations may reject or resist a proposed innovation for various reasons: because they are unaware of the need for the change; because they misinterpret the symbols used to explain the change or fail to understand its real purpose; because their customs and institutions conflict with the change; or because they are afraid of it. The target population may also resist the proposed change because they unconsciously or consciously know it is not good for them.

Cultural Resource Management (CRM) is the direction in which many archaeologists have found employment. CRM "rescues" many archaeological sites from the blades of bulldozers and other construction equipment. Several laws exist which protect archaeological materials, in recognition of their finite nature, thus creating private companies which work to properly protect this resource. This application of anthropology allows for the archaeological materials to be studied at a later time, rather than completely destroyed as used to happen in the past.

The final section of this chapter is about the newest application of anthropology; to study crime scenes or the physical remains of crime, especially the human remains of murder victims. Forensic anthropology attempts to bring together the knowledge of anatomy, physiology, taphonomy, cell biology, archaeology, and other disciplines to determine such things as identification of the victim, the criminal, or even the mode of death.

DEFINING THE GLOSSARY TERMS

Check your understanding of Chapter 17 by defining each of the glossary terms.

Applied anthropology or practicing anthropology

Cultural resource management (CRM)

Forensic anthropology

CHECK YOUR UNDERSTANDING

1. Refer to the *Applied Anthropology* box titled "Anthropology and Business." What skills do anthropologists have to offer business? What changes in business and business practices over the last couple of decades have made anthropologists necessary employees? What is an "organizational culture"? How have anthropologists been involved in studying this behavior?

2. Refer again to the *Applied Anthropology* box titled "Anthropology and Business." How has anthropologist Jill Kleinberg studied Japanese-owned firms in America? What did she discover about worker-management tensions?

3. Refer to the *Applied Anthropology* box titled "Bringing the Trees Back to Haiti." What two major uses do trees provide in Haiti? How do these two uses counter to each other? What did Gerald Murray do to alleviate this problem? Was it successful? Why?

TEST YOUR KNOWLEDGE

Select the best answer for the multiple choice questions and circle the letter T *for true and* F *for false. Short answer essay questions should be answered in full sentences and as concisely as possible.*

1. Which may involve fieldwork in order to get a broad understanding of cultural ideas and practices about health, illness, or violence? (p. 297)
   a. A social impact study
   b. Basic research
   c. Applied research
   d. Forensic research

2. Which may involve testing theories about the possible causes of specific problems? (p. 297)
   a. Social impact study
   b. Basic research
   c. Applied research
   d. Forensic research

3. Which may involve developing plans, assessing the likely social and environmental impact of particular plans, implementing the program, and monitoring the program and its effects? (p. 298)
   a. Social impact study
   b. Basic research
   c. Applied research
   d. Forensic research

4. Which involves the study, recording, and preservation of "cultural resources" that will be disturbed or destroyed by construction projects? (p. 305)
   a. Cultural resource management
   b. Basic research
   c. Applied research
   d. Forensic research

5. Which may involve the confirmation of abuses of human rights by governments? (p. 306)
   a. Social impact study
   b. Basic research
   c. Applied research
   d. Forensic research

6. T F Anthropologists who call themselves applied or practicing anthropologists are usually employed in academic settings. (p. 296)

115

7. T F Applied or practicing anthropology as a profession is explicitly concerned with making anthropological knowledge obtainable. (p. 297)

8. T F Applied anthropology in the United States developed out of anthropologists' personal experiences with disadvantaged people in other cultures. (p. 298)

9. T F An anthropologist's first responsibility is to those who employed him or her. (p. 299)

10. T F All proposed change programs are beneficial to the target population. (p. 300)

WRITE ABOUT WHAT YOU HAVE READ

11. Why are anthropologists even involved in applied anthropology? Do you think that this is appropriate? Why or why not?

12. How did applied anthropology get it real start?

13. What are the ethics of applied anthropology? Should anything be added?

14. Why is it difficult to implement planned change? What did Gerald Murray do to improve the situation in Haiti?

15. How are forensic anthropology and cultural resource management a part of the overall discipline of anthropology?

CHAPTER 18: *Medical Anthropology*

CHAPTER OUTLINE

I Cultural Understanding of Health and Illness
   A. Concepts of Balance or Equilibrium
   B. Supernatural Forces
   C. The Biomedical Paradigm

II Treatment of Illness
   A. Medical Practitioners
      1. The Shaman
      2. Physicians

III Political and Economic Influences on Health

IV Health Conditions and Diseases
   A. AIDS
   B. Mental and Emotional Disorders
   C. *Susto*
   D. Depression
   E. Undernutrition

MAJOR POINTS FOR REVIEW - CHAPTER SUMMARY

Medical anthropologists suggest that biological *and* social factors need to be considered if we are to understand how to effectively treat illness and reduce the suffering in human life.

Many of the ideas and practices of medical practitioners are influenced by the culture in which they reside. Understanding *ethnomedicine,* the medical beliefs and practices of a society or cultural group, is one of the goals of medical anthropology.

Many cultures have the view that the body should be kept in an equilibrium or balance. The balance may be between hot and cold, or wet and dry, or there may be other properties that need to be balanced.

The belief that gods or spirits can cause illness is a nearly universal. The belief in sorcery or witchcraft as a cause of illness is also very common.

Some anthropologists think that there are few cultural universals about conceptions of illness or its treatment, but some researchers are finding evidence that many of the plant remedies used by indigenous peoples contain chemicals that are the same as, or similar in effect to, chemicals used in remedies by Western biomedicine.

In the biomedical system, medical practitioners emphasize disease and cures, focusing on the body of the patient, not the mind or the social circumstances of the patient. In some societies, healers are more "personalistic" and illness may be viewed as something in one's social life being out-of-order. Shamans are perhaps the most important medical practitioners in societies lacking full-time specialization. Biomedical practitioners are becoming more aware of the psychological factors involved in healing.

People with more social, economic, and political power in a society are generally healthier. In socially stratified societies, the poor usually have increased exposure to disease because they are more likely to live in crowded and unsafe conditions and they are less likely to get access to quality care. Power and economic differentials between societies also have had profound health consequences.

The enormous death toll of AIDS, the leading cause of adult death in many countries today, will be reduced when medical science develops effective and inexpensive medicines to treat individuals with HIV or AIDS, and a vaccine to prevent individuals from getting HIV. In the meantime, if the death toll from AIDS is to be reduced, changes in attitudes, beliefs, and practices regarding sexual activity are needed.

Anthropologists debate the extent to which mental and emotional disorders are comparable across cultures. Some illnesses, such as schizophrenia and depression appear widespread enough to be universal. Others, such as *susto or anorexia nervosa,* appear to be culture-bound syndromes.

The ways that people obtain, distribute, and consume food have been generally adaptive. Geneticists have proposed that populations in famine-prone areas may have had genetic selection for "thrifty genes." Many of the serious nutritional problems of today are due to rapid cultural change, particularly those making for an increasing degree of social inequality.

DEFINING THE GLOSSARY TERMS

Check your understanding of Chapter 18 by defining each of the glossary terms.

AIDS (acquired immune deficiency syndrome)

Biomedicine

Ethnomedicine

CHECK YOUR UNDERSTANDING

1. Refer to the *Applied Anthropology* box titled "Exploring Why an Applied Project Didn't Work." What was the project? What about it wasn't working? Why? What does this say about how at least some people place value on things?

2. Refer to the *Applied Anthropology* box titled "Eating Disorders, Biology, and the Cultural Construction of Beauty." What conclusions did one of the authors discover about the perception of weight, beauty, and environment? Why does it make some kind of sense that we Americans would value thinness of obesity? How is anorexia associated with this American viewpoint? What other societies might have this disease?

3. Refer to the *Portraits of Culture* box titled "The Sagaguros of Ecuador." Illness and health can be biological and cultural. What does this statement mean? How can we apply it to our own (United States) health care system?

TEST YOUR KNOWLEDGE

Select the best answer for the multiple choice questions and circle the letter T *for true and* F *for false. Short answer essay questions should be answered in full sentences and as concisely as possible.*

1. Medical anthropologists are coming to the realization that two factors need to be considered if we are to reduce the suffering in human life? Which two? (p. 309)
   a. Social and cultural
   b. Cultural and biological
   c. Social and political
   d. Biological and social

2. The health-related beliefs, knowledge, and practices of a cultural group is called (p. 309)
   a. biocultural synthesis.
   b. its ethnomedicine.
   c. its biomedical paradigm.
   d. its concept of balance.

3. The ancient Greek system of medicine, stemming from Hippocrates, assumed that there were "humors" that must be kept in balance. What were the humors? (p. 309)
   a. Blood, phlegm, and flatulence
   b. Yellow bile, black bile, phlegm, and blood
   c. Blood, yellow bile, black bile, and flatulence
   d. Phlegm, bile, and flatulence

4. What term do most medical anthropologists use to refer to the dominant medical paradigm in Western cultures today? (p. 312)
   a. Biocultural synthesis
   b. Ethnomedicine
   c. Biomedical paradigm
   d. Biomedicine

5. The Black Death killed perhaps _____ people during the fourteenth century? (p. 316)
   a. 5 million
   b. 25 million
   c. 75 million
   d. 100 million

6. T F The Society for Medical Anthropology is now the second largest unit in the American Anthropological Association. (p. 309)

7. T F The Greek humoral medical system was dominant until it was replaced by the germ theory in the 1800's. (p. 309)

8. T F With many people around the world the belief that supernatural beings can cause illness is very uncommon. (p. 311)

9. T F Biomedicine focuses on specific diseases and cures for those diseases, rather than health. (p. 305)

10. T F Many of the serious nutritional problems of today are due to rapid cultural change, particularly the kind of change that results from increasing social inequality. (p. 321)

WRITE ABOUT WHAT YOU HAVE READ

11. Describe the biomedical paradigm. How does it apply to you personally?

12. How do shamans and physicians differ? How are they similar?

13. How are *susto* and anorexia nervosa related (in anthropology, anyway)?

14. What are the political and economic influences on health? How do these impact segments of societies?

15. What type of role can applied anthropology take in the understanding of AIDS?

CHAPTER 19: *Global Social Problems*

CHAPTER OUTLINE

I Natural Disasters and Famine

II Inadequate Housing and Homelessness

III Family Violence and Abuse
    A. Violence against Children
    B. Violence against Wives
    C. Reducing the Risk

IV Crime

V War

VI Terrorism

VII Making the World Better

MAJOR POINTS FOR REVIEW - CHAPTER SUMMARY

We may be more motivated now to try to solve social problems because worldwide communication has increased our awareness of them elsewhere, because we seem to be increasingly bothered by problems in our own society, and because we know more than we used to about various social problems that afflict our world.

The idea that we can solve global social problems is based on two assumptions. We have to assume that it is possible to discover the causes of a problem, and we have to assume that we will be able to do something about the causes once they are discovered and thereby eliminate or reduce the problem.

Disasters such as earthquakes, floods, and droughts can have greater or lesser effects on human life, depending on social conditions. Therefore disasters are partly social problems, with partly social causes and solutions.

Whether people become homeless or whether there are shantytowns, seem to depend on a society's willingness to share wealth and help those in need.

Promoting the equality of men and women and the sharing of child-rearing responsibilities may reduce family violence.

Violent crime is another area of concern here. Reducing violent crime may come down to several factors: reducing socialization and training for aggression, reduce the likelihood of war, the reduction of inequalities in wealth, and raising boys with a male role model.

Warfare is as old as society. Just the same it is now clear that the spread of more participatory political systems will lead to much less warfare. Quite often people go to war when they fear unpredictable disasters that destroy food supplies or curtail supplies of other necessities. Participatory governments alleviate these problems through internationally organized relief efforts and cause people to go to peace rather than war.

Terrorism has occurred through history. State terrorism has killed more than all wars in the twentieth century and seems to be best predicted by totalitarianism.

DEFINING THE GLOSSARY TERMS

Check your understanding of Chapter 19 by defining each of the glossary terms.

Terrorism

CHECK YOUR UNDERSTANDING

1. Refer to the *Current Research and Issues* box titled "Global Warming, Air Pollution, and Our Dependence on Oil." What reasons are listed for global warming? What does the author suggest as methods for us all to modify our behavior and thus produce less greenhouse gases? Why are we not doing what is suggested? What will probably be the ultimate answer?

2. Refer to the *Current Research and Issues* box titled "Ethnic Conflicts: Ancient Hatreds or Not?" What are Mary Kay Gilliland's observations from mid-1980s Yugoslavia? What did she see in 1991? Why do you think ethnicity became a matter of life and death to Serbs and Croats even though they had lived together harmoniously? What research questions need to be developed and implemented in order to understand this apparently growing problem?

3. Refer to the *Portraits of Culture* box titled "The Abkhazians of the Northwest Caucasus." What territorial problem exists for the Abkhazians? Is it still possible for genocide to occur in our modern world of mass communication? How?

TEST YOUR KNOWLEDGE

Select the best answer for the multiple choice questions and circle the letter T for true and F for false. Short answer essay questions should be answered in full sentences and as concisely as possible.

1. What has increased our awareness of problems all over the world? (p. 234)
   a. The increase of social problems
   b. The speed of worldwide communication
   c. Increased knowledge about human behavior
   d. More people in more societies are educated

2. The floods in the Hwang River basin have occurred mostly because of (p. 324)
   a. excessive rain.
   b. clearing of nearby forests.
   c. broken dams.
   d. a lack of engineering skill.

3. What did people in the past, and even recently in some places, view as divine retribution for human immorality? (p. 325)
   a. Natural disasters
   b. Famine
   c. Poverty
   d. AIDS

4. As of the 1980s, ____ percent of the population in Nairobi, Kenya lived in unauthorized housing.? (p. 326)
   a. 10
   b. 20
   c. 40
   d. 60

5. Most researchers agree that _____ involves the threat or use of violence against civilians. (p. 334)
   a. natural disasters
   b. war
   c. terrorism
   d. family violence and abuse

6. T F Natural disasters are social problems. (p. 324)

7. T F The people of a society are all equally at risk in case of disaster. (p. 324)

8. T F All dwellers in illegal settlements are poor. (p. 326)

9. T F The deliberate policy to reduce the number of people hospitalized for mental illness and other disabilities is a factor that causes homelessness in the U.S. (p. 327)

10. T F Cross-culturally, many societies practice and allow infanticide. (p. 329)

WRITE ABOUT WHAT YOU HAVE READ

11. Why is applied anthropology so interested in natural disasters and famine?

12. Define the concept of inadequate housing. Does this vary culturally? How?

13. What is family violence? What are the typical patterns? What can be done to alleviate family violence?

14. What is crime? In what types of societies is it a real problem? How do various types of societies deal with it?

15. Warfare has apparently always existed. It is even practiced by chimpanzees on some very small scale (at least murder is). So can warfare be eliminated? How? Can we really make the world better?

TEST YOUR KNOWLEDGE ANSWER KEY

Chapter 1
1. d 2. c 3. d 4. a 5. b 6. T 7. F 8. F 9. F 10. T 11. F 12. F 13. T

Chapter 2
1. c 2. b 3. d 4. b 5. c 6. F 7. F 8. T 9. F 10. T 11. F 12. F 13. T

Chapter 3
1. d 2. c 3. b 4. c 5. b 6. T 7. T 8. T 9. F 10. T 11. F 12. T 13. T

Chapter 4
1. b 2. c 3. d 4. b 5. b 6. F 7. F 8. F 9. T 10. T

Chapter 5
1. a 2. b 3. d 4. c 5. d 6. T 7. F 8. F 9. T 10. F

Chapter 6
1. d 2. d 3. c 4. b 5. a 6. F 7. F 8. F 9. F 10. F

Chapter 7
1. b 2. c 3. d 4. c 5. a 6. F 7. T 8. T 9. F 10. F

Chapter 8
1. b 2. a 3. c 4. c 5. c 6. T 7. F 8. F 9. T 10. T

Chapter 9
1. d 2. d 3. c 4. a 5. b 6. T 7. F 8. T 9. F 10. F

Chapter 10
1. b 2. d 3. c 4. a 5. d 6. F 7. F 8. T 9. T 10. F

Chapter 11
1. c 2. a 3. b 4. c 5. a 6. T 7. F 8. T 9. F 10. F

Chapter 12
1. c 2. a 3. c 4. d 5. b 6. T 7. T 8. T 9. F 10. T

Chapter 13
1. a 2. c 3. d 4. c 5. a 6. T 7. T 8. F 9. F 10. T

Chapter 14
1. c 2. a 3. b 4. d 5. b 6. T 7. F 8. F 9. T 10. T

Chapter 15
1. a 2. d 3. c 4. d 5. d 6. T 7. T 8. T 9. F 10. F

Chapter 16
1. b 2. d 3. c 4. a 5. d 6. F 7. F 8. T 9. F 10. T 11. T

Chapter 17
1. b 2. b 3. c 4. a 5. d 6. F 7. F 8. T 9. F 10. F

Chapter 18
1. d 2. b 3. b 4. d 5. c 6. T 7. F 8. F 9. T 10. T

Chapter 19
1. b 2. b 3. a 4. c 5. c 6. T 7. F 8. F 9. T 10. T